HIDDEN HISTORY
OF
TWIN CITIES
SPORTS

HIDDEN HISTORY
OF
TWIN CITIES SPORTS

JOEL RIPPEL

THE
History
PRESS

Published by The History Press
Charleston, SC
www.historypress.com

Front cover, top left: University of Minnesota; *top right*: University of Minnesota; *bottom left*: Minnesota Twins; *bottom right*: National Basketball Association. *Back cover, left*: Minnesota Pipers; *middle*: University of Minnesota; *right*: Minnesota Twins.

First published 2023

Manufactured in the United States

ISBN 9781467153188

Library of Congress Control Number: 2022951602

Notice: The information in this book is true and complete to the best of our knowledge. It is offered without guarantee on the part of the author or The History Press. The author and The History Press disclaim all liability in connection with the use of this book.

For Sophie

CONTENTS

CONTENTS

PREFACE

The Twin Cities became home to a Major League Baseball team and a National Football League team in 1961. Both teams became tenants of Metropolitan Stadium in suburban Bloomington. Less than ten years later, talk began about replacing Metropolitan Stadium, which had opened in 1956. By the mid-1970s, that talk, first heard in 1969, had become a heated debate.

In April 1975, Minnesota governor Wendell Anderson announced that he was convinced that both the Minnesota Twins and the Minnesota Vikings would leave the state unless a new stadium was built.

On March 28, 1976, Senator Hubert Humphrey, a former mayor of Minneapolis, expressed his concern about the topic. He urged the Minnesota House Democratic-Farmer-Labor Party (DFL) caucus to support a new stadium and pass stadium legislation. "Great sports events are good for this community and are the best way to make Minnesota known to the rest of the country," Humphrey said. "Don't miss the chance to give this state an opportunity to move forward. We can't afford to do less." He added that without professional sports, the Twin Cities would be just a "cold Omaha."

A year later, the Minnesota legislature passed a bill that led to the building of a domed stadium in downtown Minneapolis. The stadium, which opened in 1982, was named after Humphrey, who died in 1978 at the age of sixty-seven.

While the Twin Cities sports scene most likely would have been significantly altered if the Hubert H. Humphrey Metrodome had not been built, the rich history of sports in the Twin Cities would not have been diminished.

Sports such as baseball, curling and lacrosse were being played in the Twin Cities before Minnesota became a state in 1858. In the late nineteenth century, the Twin Cities played a role in the development of basketball, boxing and golf nationally. In the twentieth century, Minnesota made contributions to college football and hockey that enjoyed nationwide attention.

While much of that history has been acknowledged in print, there have been stories that haven't received the attention they deserved. The goal of this book is to bring some of those stories and some of Minnesota's sporting pioneers to light.

ACKNOWLEDGEMENTS

I am grateful to John Rodrigue of The History Press for the opportunity to work on this project. Without John's patience, direction and understanding, this project could not and would not have been completed.

As a member of the Society for American Baseball Research (SABR), a national organization founded in 1971 with more than six thousand members, I was able to utilize resources made available by the organization on numerous occasions.

I haven't met anyone who knows more about Minnesota sports history than Patrick Reusse and Stew Thornley. Patrick, a Twin Cities sports journalist for more than fifty years, and Stew, a SABR member who has written extensively about Minnesota sports, were quick to answer my questions.

While working on this project, I received help and support from many people.

Michelle Traversie and Brad Rempel of the University of Minnesota Athletic Communications office were very supportive of the project and provided pictures.

Others who provided photo assistance were Eric Tabor, from the University of Montana Athletic Communications office; David Nelson, director of sports information programs for Hamline University; Chisholm (Minnesota) High School activities director Travis Vake; and Dustin Morse, senior director of communications for the Minnesota Twins, and Molly Kaiser, an intern with the Twins.

L.J. COOKE

THE STATE OF BASKETBALL

Minnesota is home to the U.S. Hockey Hall of Fame in Eveleth and is known as the "State of Hockey" for its role in the development of the sport in the United States.

Minnesota should also be recognized for its role in the spread and development of basketball in the United States. In 1891, Dr. James Naismith, shortly after he became the director of the YMCA in Springfield, Massachusetts, invented an indoor activity to be played during the winter months to fill the void between the football and baseball seasons.

The game spread through the YMCA network and quickly became popular in Minnesota because of two of Naismith's protégés. The first was Max Exner, who had been a roommate of Naismith's in Springfield and participated in the first basketball game, on December 21, 1891. Exner brought the game to Carleton College in Northfield, Minnesota, in the winter of 1892–93 after becoming the school's first instructor of "physical culture" and the director of gymnastics at the school.

The other student of Naismith was Louis Joseph "L.J." Cooke. Cooke spent two summer sessions at the Springfield YMCA studying under Naismith before earning a medical degree at the University of Vermont.

In 1895, the twenty-seven-year-old Cooke became the director of physical education at the Minneapolis YMCA. The next year, he became the basketball coach for the University of Minnesota on a part-time basis while still working at the YMCA.

In the fall of 1897, Cooke accepted the university's offer of a full-time position as director of the school's physical education program and as the basketball coach. This made Cooke, a native of Toledo, Ohio, one of the first full-time basketball coaches in the country.

He quickly developed the Gophers basketball program into one of the best in the nation in the first two decades of the twentieth century. Between February 1901 and January 1904, Cooke coached the Gophers to 34 consecutive victories, including unbeaten seasons in 1901–2 and 1902–3. The Big Ten Conference offered basketball as a sport for the first time in the 1905–6 season. The Gophers went 6-1 against conference foes to earn the Big Ten's first basketball title. The Gophers were conference co-champions (with the University of Chicago) in 1906–7.

Dr. Louis Joseph "L.J." Cooke began coaching basketball at the University of Minnesota in 1896. *University of Minnesota.*

In the 1910–11 season, the Gophers were co-champions (with Purdue) and won conference titles in the 1916–17 and 1918–19 seasons.

Cooke retired from coaching following the 1923–24 season to become the athletic department's ticket manager. According to athletic department records, he had a career coaching record of 250-135.

Even though national college basketball Top 25 polls didn't begin until 1948 (nine years after the first NCAA men's national tournament), several of Cooke's Gophers teams have been retroactively named national champions.

The 1901–2 team was named national champion by both the Helms Athletic Foundation and in the Premo-Porretta Power Poll. The 1902–3 team was also named national champion by the Premo-Porretta Poll. The 1918–19 team, which went 13-0 overall and 10-0 in the conference, was named national champion by both entities.

In 1943, the Helms Athletic Foundation, based in Los Angeles, retroactively named a national champion for the years 1900 to 1941. Minnesota was named champs for the 1901–2 and 1918–19 seasons by the foundation.

In 1995, the Premo-Porretta Power Poll, started by Patrick Premo, a college professor, and Phil Porretta, a former computer programmer, ranked college basketball teams retroactively from the 1895–96 through the 1947–48 seasons.

The University of Minnesota began playing basketball in its current arena in 1928. The first game in the University of Minnesota Field House was on February 4, 1928. Among the speakers at the first game in the new facility, which cost $650,000 to build ($11.26 million in 2022 terms) and was renamed Williams Arena in 1950, was Naismith.

Naismith, then a professor at the University of Kansas, spoke to the crowd of eleven thousand, which the *Minneapolis Tribune* described as the largest basketball crowd to ever attend an intercollegiate basketball game in the "northwest." In his brief halftime speech, he said, "The occasion that called me to the center of the floor to start this game tonight takes me back 36 years when I stepped to the center of a floor less than one-third the size of the court before you, to start the world's first basketball game.

"It is phenomenal that the game should spread so within the life of a single individual. The University of Minnesota was one of the pioneers in the game of basketball and its early start in the game was directed by lifelong friend, Dr. L.J. Cooke."

After becoming the ticket manager in 1924, Cooke continued to serve as assistant director of physical education and assistant director in the athletic department until retiring in 1936. In 1938, the school named its athletic administration building, which had opened in 1934, Cooke Hall.

Cooke passed away in August 1943 at his home in Minneapolis just several blocks from the university campus. He was seventy-five. At the time of his death, he held a professor emeritus title from the university.

The *Minneapolis Daily Times* reported in its August 19, 1943 edition that in his capacity as a lecturer in the physical education department, "Doc Cooke probably created a more lasting impression on the student body than in any other. Thousands of alumni remember vividly the doctor's colorful personal-hygiene lectures. Pungent, pointed and witty, these discussions were, and are, still widely quoted wherever students of the doctor gather."

The newspaper said that the pallbearers at his funeral would be members of the "famous undefeated Minnesota basketball team of 1919."

Cooke's impact on the game is undeniable. While coaching and teaching at the University of Minnesota, he was a member of the rules committee, which oversaw the sport nationally.

The Big Ten Conference men's basketball record book credits Minnesota with eight conference championships, five of which were coached by Cooke. Since the Gophers' unbeaten 1918–19 season, the program has won conference titles in 1937, 1972 and 1982. The Gophers also won the conference title in the 1996–97 season, but that title was later vacated because of NCAA sanctions.

THE TWIN CITIES AND THE AMERICAN LEAGUE, VERSION 1.0

After several major-league franchises flirted with the idea of moving to the Twin Cities in the 1950s, the Washington Senators announced that they would relocate to Minnesota following the 1960 season and begin play in 1961.

But the 1961 season wasn't the first time the Twin Cities had been associated with the American League or Major League Baseball.

The Twin Cities' first exposure to "major-league" baseball occurred in 1884. That year, the area fielded three teams—Minneapolis, St. Paul and Stillwater—in the minor-league Northwestern League. One of the players on the Stillwater team was Bud Fowler, who is the earliest known African American to play in organized professional baseball. Fowler was enshrined in the National Baseball Hall of Fame in Cooperstown, New York, in 2022.

The Northwestern League consisted of fourteen teams based in the Midwest. Only two teams—Milwaukee and St. Paul—were able to complete the season. The league ceased operations on September 7, four days after the Minneapolis team folded.

But that wasn't the end of the season for the Milwaukee and St. Paul teams. In late September, the teams were invited to join the upstart Union Association. The league was considered a major league, along with the National League and the American Association.

The St. Paul team played its first Union Association game on September 27. Over the next three weeks, St. Paul played 9 games, all on the road (in

Cincinnati, Kansas City and St. Louis). St. Paul played its final game on October 13 in Kansas City.

The brief foray into the Union Association allowed three St. Paul players to become the first native Minnesotans to play in the major leagues. Bill Barnes (born in Shakopee), Lou Galvin (born in St. Paul) and Joe Werrick (born in St. Paul) played for St. Paul in the Union Association games. For Barnes and Galvin, it was their only major-league experience. Werrick would later spend three seasons with Louisville of the American Association. Barnes and Werrick made their major-league debuts in St. Paul's first Union Association game on September 27; Galvin made his on October 1.

Another member of the St. Paul team in 1884, Minneapolis native Elmer Foster, did not play in the 9 Union Association games because he was injured. In late August, while pitching against Milwaukee in St. Paul, Foster suffered a broken arm on the first pitch of the game. A month earlier, on July 31, Foster pitched a ten-inning no-hitter in St. Paul's 2–1 victory at Milwaukee. Foster struck out 13 in the victory. The injury forced him to miss the rest of the 1884 season and all of 1885. But in 1886, he made it to the majors with the (New York) Metropolitans of the American Association. He played with two teams in the National League from 1888 to 1891.

Joe Visner, a Minneapolis native and member of the Stillwater team in the Northwestern League in 1884, made his major-league debut with Baltimore of the American Association in 1885 and spent four seasons in the big leagues.

After the failure of the Northwestern League in 1884, there was no professional baseball in the Twin Cities in 1885. The Northwestern League returned in 1886 and 1887, and in 1888, Minneapolis and St. Paul both joined the Western League. Except for two interruptions—neither city had a team in 1893, and St. Paul didn't field a team in 1894—the Twin Cities teams remained in the Western League until 1899.

The Twin Cities did receive one more exposure to Major League Baseball on October 2, 1891, when Columbus and Milwaukee, of the American Association, played a game at Athletic Park in downtown Minneapolis. Milwaukee defeated Columbus, 5–0.

Among the players on the Columbus roster was St. Paul native Jack Crooks, one of the earliest Minnesota natives to play in the major leagues. Crooks played in the majors from 1889 to 1898.

It was the only regular-season major-league game played in Minnesota prior to the Twins' inaugural season in 1961. Columbus and Milwaukee were scheduled to play a second game in Minneapolis on October 3, but the game was called off because of cold weather. The teams returned to Milwaukee for their season finale on October 4. The American Association, which operated from 1884 to 1891, ceased operations after the season.

Following the 1894 Western League season, Charles Comiskey purchased the Sioux City (Iowa) Western League team and moved it to St. Paul. Within five years, Comiskey and Western League president Ban Johnson would move to make the Western League a "major" league.

In October 1899, the Western League changed its name to the American League. The league made two franchise moves: It purchased a vacant ballpark in Cleveland and moved the Grand Rapids franchise there, and it allowed Comiskey to move the St. Paul franchise to Chicago.

Comiskey's Chicago White Sox won the 1900 American League pennant with an 82-53 record. The Minneapolis Millers finished last in the standings with a 53-86 record and was last in attendance (about 71,000).

After the 1900 season, Johnson initiated his bold plan to make the American League the equal of the "major" National League. In October 1900, the AL announced its intention to expand. It said it would put teams in "vacant" territories in the East. For the next couple of months, there was a lot of uncertainty about the future of professional baseball in Minneapolis and St. Paul, which did not field a team in 1900.

On November 25, the *Minneapolis Tribune* reported, "About the only thing that seems sure is that it [Minneapolis] will be summarily fired from the American League."

A story in the December 19, 1900 edition of the *Minneapolis Journal* with the headline "Fans in Suspense" reported that Minneapolis could field two professional teams in 1901, in the Western League and in the just-formed Western Association. Three days later, the *Minneapolis Daily Times* said that the Minneapolis team was expected "to be cut out of the American League."

On December 24, the *Daily Times* reported that Minneapolis would officially be in the Western League in 1901. St. Paul would also have a team in the league in 1901.

The American League soon made it official when it said that it would put teams in Baltimore, Boston, Philadelphia and Washington, D.C., in 1901. Those cities would replace Buffalo, Indianapolis, Kansas City and Minneapolis.

The 1901 season was the first year that the American League was officially classified as a "major" league. After that season, Minneapolis and St. Paul left the Western League and joined the newly formed American Association, where they would remain until 1960.

In October 1960, the American League approved a move by the Washington Senators to Minnesota. The Washington team, one of the clubs that had replaced Minneapolis in the AL in 1900, began play as the Minnesota Twins in 1961.

A special preview section was included in the April 16, 1961 edition of the *Minneapolis Sunday Tribune*. A headline on a story written by Dick Cullum summed up the state's complicated story with major-league baseball: "Minneapolis Has Been Big League Before—Briefly."

3

FRANK FORCE

AN IMPACT ON TWIN CITIES SPORTSWRITING

A fter graduating from Minneapolis North High School in the mid-1890s, Frank E. Force had an eclectic life.

After high school, he served in the Thirteenth Minnesota Regiment in the Philippine-American War. After surviving a life-threatening bout of typhoid fever during the war, he returned to Minneapolis, where he earned a bachelor of arts degree in literature in 1900 and a master's in literature the next year from the University of Minnesota.

In April 1903, at the age of twenty-four, Force became the "sporting" editor of the *Minneapolis Tribune*. Even though his tenure as the *Tribune*'s sports editor lasted only until 1914—it included a one-year leave of absence—Force would have a connection to sports journalism in Minneapolis for over one hundred years.

Force, who had started his career at the *Tribune* as a news reporter, was the newspaper's first sports editor.

The first newspapers in Minnesota began publishing during the state's territorial years (1849–58). The *Minneapolis Tribune* began publishing in 1867, the same year Minneapolis incorporated as a city.

Sporting events in the state date to the territorial years—or earlier—as well. Lacrosse was played as early as 1836 at Fort Snelling. The first baseball game in the state was played in 1857, the year before statehood. The first state baseball tournament was held in 1867, and boxing matches were held in the state as early as 1876.

The University of Minnesota, which was founded in Minneapolis in 1851, fielded its first baseball team in 1876 and its first football squad in 1882.

In the second half of the nineteenth century, the state's newspapers didn't report much on sporting events. That changed in the first years of the twentieth century, as newspapers in Minneapolis and St. Paul provided more sports coverage. Seven months after Force was named the sports editor, the *Minneapolis Tribune* announced expanded sports coverage in the newspaper: "Recognizing the importance of the sporting interests of the greater Northwest, it has been decided that a whole section of the *Sunday Tribune* will hereafter be devoted to news of this character. It will be under the personal supervision of the well-known Sporting Editor Frank E. Force and will be better and more extensive than anything ever attempted by a newspaper outside of New York and Chicago, and, as a matter of fact it promises to be just a little bit more readable than any sporting supplement published. It will make its first appearance next Sunday [December 6]."

Over the next few years, Force covered several big events in the Twin Cities.

The Gophers football team won 42 of 45 games between 1903 and 1906. The record included a tie game with Michigan in 1903. That game was the start of the teams' Little Brown Jug rivalry.

Dan Patch, a horse-racing legend, set a world record at the 1906 Minnesota State Fair, and the 1909 Minneapolis Millers won 107 games while winning the American Association title.

In October 1909, Force was granted a leave of absence from the *Tribune* to pursue a "business opportunity" in Asia. He traveled to Borneo, where he arranged to bring a group of forty-five Dyak tribesmen on a tour of the United States. The *Minneapolis Tribune* described the group as the "proverbial wildmen of Borneo."

Force took the group to several U.S. national parks and state fairs, including the Minnesota State Fair, in 1910. In 1911, he returned to his job as sports editor.

Force left the *Tribune* in 1914. Among the jobs he held after college were baseball umpire, boxing referee and promoter, radio announcer, real estate agent, English teacher and president of a professional baseball league.

Shortly before he left the newspaper, he hired a sixteen-year-old high school student named Charles Johnson as a "cub" reporter.

Johnson was named the sports editor of the *Minneapolis Star* in 1920 at the age of twenty-two. His journalism career spanned more than fifty years, primarily as the executive sports editor of the *Star* and the *Minneapolis Tribune*. In 1948, after the *Minneapolis Times* (a sister publication of the

Minneapolis Tribune) folded, Johnson hired Dick Cullum and Sid Hartman. Cullum wrote for the *Tribune* until 1982. Hartman wrote for the *Tribune* (and *Star Tribune*) until October 2020. Hartman's last column in the *Star Tribune* appeared the day he passed away, October 18, seven months after his one hundredth birthday.

Force died in March 1964 at the age of eighty-five. He was buried at Fort Rosecrans National Cemetery in San Diego, California.

After Force's death, Johnson wrote in the March 27, 1964 edition of the *Minneapolis Star*, "He was a colorful figure on the local sports front for many years."

4

PERRY WERDEN

PROFESSIONAL BASEBALL'S FIRST SLUGGER

Late in the 1920 baseball season, Babe Ruth, in his first year with the New York Yankees, hit his 46th home run of the campaign to set a new single-season record for all of organized baseball. The new record was especially newsworthy in Minneapolis, even though the closest major-league teams were four hundred miles away in Chicago.

Ruth, who finished the 1920 season with 54 home runs, had broken the record of 45, set twenty-five years earlier by Perry Werden of the minor-league Minneapolis Millers. The headline in the September 5, 1920 issue of the *Minneapolis Sunday Tribune* read: "Babe Ruth Smacks Out Two More as Yanks Divide. Perry Werden's Record Is Shoved into Discard."

Werden had set the record of 45 in 1895. That total surpassed the previous record of 43, set by Werden with the Millers in 1894.

In 1894, the Millers and Werden, who was in his first season in Minneapolis after being released by St. Louis of the major-league American Association, played their home games in Athletic Park in downtown Minneapolis. The compact ballpark was located on the site where the Butler Square building stands today, just one block from Target Field, the current home of the Minnesota Twins.

Werden and the Millers benefited from the cozy dimensions (just 250 feet down the right- and left-field foul lines). Werden batted .417 that season and hit 37 of his home runs at Athletic Park. His 43 home runs surpassed the organized baseball record of 31—also hit in 1894—by Buck Freeman of Haverhill in the New England League. The Millers finished in fourth place in the eight-team league with a 63-62 record.

The six-foot, two-inch, 220-pound Werden, who had made his professional debut in 1884 by going 12-1 as a pitcher for St. Louis of the major-league Union Association, had a better offensive season in 1895.

He started the campaign by going 8-for-13 in the Millers' sweep of their season-opening 3-game series in Milwaukee. After 10 games, Werden was batting .553 (26-for-47).

On July 4, Werden went 0-for-5 in the Millers' 14–8 loss to the St. Paul Apostles in the second game of a doubleheader. That was the last time for nearly seven weeks that Werden didn't get at least 1 hit in a game. After the loss to the Apostles, the Millers embarked on an 11-game road trip.

On July 6, Werden had 2 hits in the Millers' 12–11 victory over Grand Rapids in Michigan. That started a 40-game hitting streak for Werden.

In back-to-back home games on July 22–23, Werden went 9-for-9 with 6 home runs. He went 4-for-4 with 2 home runs in a 17–8 loss to Indianapolis. The next day, he went 5-for-5 and drove in 9 runs with 4 home runs and 1 single.

On July 27, he hit a 2-run home run in the Millers' 19–7 victory over Grand Rapids. That victory started a 9-game winning streak for the Millers. Werden went 24-for-49 during the streak.

The hitting streak came to an end on August 20, when he went 0-for-3 in the Millers' 5–0 loss to Kansas City. During the streak, he hit 18 home runs and batted .477 (94-for-197).

On September 17, in a 25–15 victory over Grand Rapids, he hit his 44th home run of the season to eclipse his 1894 total. Two days later, he went 5-for-6 with his 45th homer. Werden hit safely in the Millers' final 18 games of the season and finished the campaign with a league-leading .428 batting average. He tied for the league lead in hits (241) with St. Paul's Bill George. As a team, the Millers hit 219 home runs in 123 games.

Werden's hitting streak, which wasn't mentioned in newspaper accounts while it was ongoing, isn't included in a list of longest hitting streaks in minor-league history. That list doesn't include any pre-1900 streaks. Since 1900, there have been only sixteen longer hitting streaks in minor-league baseball.

One of those streaks is disputed. In 1912, newspapers reported that Jack Lelivelt of Rochester in the International League hit safely in his 40th consecutive game. One newspaper account described Lelivelt's feat as "what is believed to be a record for consecutive hitting never before approached in a minor-league and being on par with Tyrus Raymond Cobb of the Detroit Tigers last year in the American League."

According to Lelivelt's biography on the Society for American Baseball Research's website, his hitting streak was 33 games. The author of the biography looked at Rochester's box scores day by day and found a 33-game streak between April 23 and June 3 that season. The International League record book credits his streak as 42 games.

By comparison, there were two hitting streaks of more than 40 games in the major leagues in the 1890s. Bill Dahlen hit in 42 consecutive games with the Chicago Colts of the National League in 1894, and Willie Keeler hit in 45 consecutive games for the NL's Baltimore Orioles spanning the 1896 and 1897 seasons. He hit safely in the final game of the 1896 season and in his first 44 games in 1897.

Werden's record-breaking season is credited with stabilizing professional baseball in Minneapolis. Since the city had fielded its first fully professional team in the Northwestern League in 1884, there had been two seasons (1885 and 1893) without a professional team in Minneapolis and three seasons (1888, 1891 and 1892) in which a Minneapolis team did not complete the season because of financial difficulties.

In 1896, the Millers played their first 17 home games at Athletic Park before moving into a new park just south of downtown Minneapolis. Werden, who had hit 7 home runs at Athletic Park before the move to the larger Nicollet Park, finished the season with 18 home runs to lead the Western League in that category for the third consecutive season.

Werden left the Millers in 1897 to play for the Louisville Colonels of the National League but rejoined the Millers in 1898. He continued his playing career until 1908. In twenty-four seasons of professional baseball, he had 2,897 hits and 195 home runs.

Werden passed away in January 1934. The headline in the *Minneapolis Tribune* read, "Perry Werden, Holder of Home Run Record for Over 20 Years Succumbs to Heart Attack at 69."

George Barton, a sportswriter and columnist in Minneapolis for fifty-five years (1903–58), wrote: "Baseball lost one of its most famous and loveable characters in the death of Perry Wheritt Werden. Old time ballplayers who saw Werden ruin pitchers said that he was Babe Ruth's equal, if not his superior."

The *Post-Dispatch*, in Werden's hometown of St. Louis, wrote, "Perry Werden 'Babe Ruth of Nineties' Dies."

Donie Bush, the Millers' manager at the time, said, "Werden was one of the greatest hitters of all time." And Alfred H. Spink wrote in *The National Game* about Werden, "In his day, he was a fine first baseman as well as one of the hardest hitters in the business."

5

EVELYNE HALL, ANN GOVEDNIK

MINNESOTA'S FIRST FEMALE ATHLETES AT A SUMMER OLYMPICS

Evelyne Hall started her running career as a youth in South Minneapolis. She went on to become a women's pioneer in the sport of track and field. From those early experiences in races at church picnics, Hall went on to become the first woman from Minnesota to earn an Olympic medal when she competed in the 1932 Olympics in Los Angeles.

The first Minnesota-born athlete to compete at the Olympics was J. Ira Courtney, who competed in three track-and-field events at the 1912 Olympics in Stockholm, Sweden. The 1912 games were the fifth "modern" Olympics to be held. The first was in Athens, Greece, in 1896. Courtney, a student at the University of Washington in 1912, is also considered the first Olympian from the Pacific Northwest.

At the 1920 Olympics in Antwerp, Belgium, Frank Loomis, who was born in St. Paul in 1896, became the first Minnesotan to earn a gold medal when he won the 400-meter hurdle race. Loomis served as the coach of the U.S. Olympic women's track team at the 1932 games.

One of the highlights of the 1932 Olympics was Hall's race against Babe Didrikson in the 80-meter hurdles event on August 4. Didrikson edged Hall for the gold medal with a world-record time of 11.7 seconds. In an interview with the *Los Angeles Times* in July 1988, Hall said, "To this day, it is still remembered as the most controversial race in the Olympics."

Hall admitted in the interview that she was nervous before the race, "I was paralyzed. I went down to the [stadium] floor, and I was so wobbly, I couldn't stand. I looked at those thousands and thousands of people and I felt like a wet noodle. My legs buckled, my arms too."

As was the standard then, hurdlers "dug" a starting hole instead of a using a starting block, as is done today. Hall said she couldn't even dig her own hole. "I just sat on this chair," Hall said, "Someone else had to dig it for me."

The race was also memorable because it was the first time an electric-eye camera was used at the finish line. It was considered experimental, and judges at the finish line had the final say.

Hall and Didrikson hit the finish line simultaneously. It was so close that the finish was reviewed. Photos from several angles were inconclusive. Thirty minutes after the race, the official judge declared Didrikson the winner.

"My teammates yelled 'you've won,'" Hall told the *Minneapolis Star Tribune* in 1988. When asked by a *Star Tribune* reporter if she thought she had won the race, Hall said, "Yes, I did. I didn't protest. I'm not that kind of protest. I didn't want to take away anything from Babe."

Talk about the race's finish lingered. Several days later, when the finish of the men's 100-meter race was close, both races were reviewed again. Hall told the *Los Angeles Times* that after the second review, Olympic officials "declared that the least I had done was tied [with Didrikson]."

Hall said that Olympic officials "hinted that had she and Didrikson been from different countries, a protest would have been filed. But because teammates were involved a protest was denied."

After the 1932 Olympics, Hall won American indoor titles in the 80-meter hurdles in 1933 and 1935. She was a candidate for the 1936 Olympic team, which competed at the Berlin games. But the financially strapped U.S. Olympic Committee expected athletes to pay $1,000 out of their own pockets toward the travel costs to Germany. Hall couldn't afford it.

She went on to coach the first U.S. women's track-and-field team to compete in the Pan American Games, in 1951. She later served as the chairperson for the U.S. Olympic women's track-and-field team.

About two months shy of her seventy-fifth birthday, she carried the ceremonial Olympic torch through Carlsbad, California, on its way to Los Angeles for the 1984 Summer Olympics.

Hall, whose married name was Adams, died in April 1983 after suffering a heart attack. Hall Adams, who also worked as the recreation director for the city of Gardena, California, was eighty-three.

In the 1988 interview with the *Minneapolis Star Tribune*, she reflected on her career: "I feel as if I'm a pioneer."

Hall Adams, who was named to the USA Track and Field Hall of Fame in 1988, wasn't the only pioneer from Minneapolis at the 1932 Olympics. She was joined by a sixteen-year-old swimmer from Chisholm on Minnesota's Iron Range.

Ann Govednik finished in sixth place in the 200-meter breaststroke in a race in which Australian Claire Dennis set a world record. It was Govednik's first of two Olympics. She also competed four years later at the Berlin Olympics.

Govednik had started swimming competitively for Chisholm High School two years earlier. The Iron Range was a mecca for girls' high school swimming in the state. A girls' state swimming meet was held on the Iron Range from 1924 to 1942. The 1942 meet was the last one for girls in Minnesota—in any sport—until 1972.

At the 1932 state meet, Govednik won the 100-meter breaststroke event with a time that broke the U.S. high school record. Two weeks after the meet, she broke the Amateur Athletic Union (AAU) world record for the event at the AAU national meet in New York City.

At the 1932 U.S. Olympic swimming trials, Govednik finished second in the 200-meter backstroke to qualify for the U.S. Olympic team. Govednik turned sixteen as she traveled with the U.S. swim team on a seventeen-car "special" train from New York to Los Angeles for the Olympics.

In 1936, Govednik developed a serious ear infection while on board the SS *Manhattan* crossing the Atlantic. After arriving in Berlin, she spent some time in a hospital before competing in the 200-meter qualifying event. She didn't advance to the finals.

She earned degrees in physical education and English from St. Cloud State in 1939 and began her coaching and teaching career in Little Falls, Minnesota. She taught swimming at the University of Minnesota–Duluth and taught physical education and swimming at a junior high school in Duluth for seventeen years before retiring in 1975.

Govednik, whose married named was Van Steinburg, died in August 1985 in Duluth at the age of sixty-nine. She is a member of the Minnesota Swimming Coaches Hall of Fame and the St. Cloud State Athletic Hall of Fame.

Six months before the 1932 Summer Olympics, the first female Minnesotans to compete in a Winter Olympics participated in the 1932 games in Lake Placid, New York. Margaret Bennett of Minneapolis competed in figure skating and Dorothy Franey Langkop of St. Paul in speed skating. Franey Langkop finished third in the "non-medal" 1,000-meter race.

6

LIGHTS TURNED OUT ON
PRO BASKETBALL IN ST. PAUL

The early history of professional basketball in the Twin Cities is dominated by the accomplishments of the Minneapolis Lakers. The team began play in 1947 and, in the first seven years of existence, won six league championships (in three different leagues).

That success overshadowed two attempts at professional basketball in St. Paul.

In the fall of 1947, there were four professional basketball leagues in the United States: the American Basketball League (formed in 1925), the National Basketball League (1935), the Basketball Association of America (1946) and the Professional Basketball League of America (1947).

The Professional Basketball League of America (PBLA) came into existence when Maurice White, the owner of the Chicago American Gears, announced that after three seasons in the National Basketball League (NBL) he was pulling his team out of the league to form the PBLA. The Gears' departure from the NBL came after they had won the 1947 NBL title, primarily because of the efforts of a talented rookie named George Mikan.

The newly formed PBLA had sixteen teams in two eight-team divisions. The Gears were in the Northern Division along with Grand Rapids (Michigan), Kansas City, Louisville, Omaha, St. Joseph (Missouri), Waterloo (Iowa) and St. Paul.

Bruce Hale, who had been a collegiate star at Santa Clara and played for the Gears, was named the player-coach for the St. Paul team. One of the first players signed by the franchise was Marty Passaglia, an All-

American at Santa Clara before playing with Washington in the Basketball Association of America.

The St. Paul team opened its season on October 27, 1947, with a 55–49 victory over Waterloo in Iowa. Hale scored 14 points to lead St. Paul. The team won 6 of its first 9 games.

On November 12, St. Paul lost to Kansas City, 39–34, in a game played in Tulsa, Oklahoma. That would be the team's last game. While the team was returning to the Twin Cities, the league announced that it was canceling all remaining games and was disbanding.

St. Paul, along with the Gears, which won all 9 games they played, and Atlanta, which was in the Southern Division and won 7 of its 8 games, were considered the league's top teams.

James O. Brooks, an attorney for the league, told the *Chicago Tribune* in its November 13, 1947 edition that the reason for canceling the season was "that the league attendance has been financially unsuccessful."

According to a report in the *Minneapolis Tribune*, St. Paul had drawn just five thousand fans with gate receipts of just $4,000 in its 2 home games. The Associated Press reported that the league's teams had lost a combined $600,000 ($7.97 million in 2022) in its first month.

The PBLA's demise was good news to the Minneapolis Lakers. All of the league's 160 players became free agents, and the Lakers signed Mikan. The Lakers also considered signing Bruce Hale, but he joined Indianapolis of the NBL.

Following the closure of the PBLA, there was more change in professional basketball's landscape. In 1949, the BAA and NBL merged to become the National Basketball Association (NBA). The Lakers, with Mikan, had won the NBL title in 1948, the BAA title in 1949 and would win four titles in their first five seasons in the NBA.

In 1950, another professional basketball league was formed, primarily by NBL teams that had not joined the NBA. The National Professional Basketball League, which began play in the fall of 1950, had eight teams, including the St. Paul Lights.

The second attempt at professional basketball in St. Paul lasted only slightly longer than the attempt of three years earlier.

The Lights named former Hamline basketball star Howie Schultz its player-coach. Schultz was in the first year of his professional basketball career after spending the previous five years playing major-league baseball. Schultz, a native of St. Paul, is one of just thirteen athletes documented to have played professional basketball and major-league baseball.

The St. Paul roster featured another former Hamline basketball star, Hal Haskins. In high school, Haskins was a standout for Alexandria (Minnesota) High School and helped the Cardinals reach the championship game of the 1943 state basketball tournament. The Cardinals lost to St. Paul Washington in the championship game, but Haskins averaged 19 points per game in three state tournament games, the second most up to that point in state tournament history. Haskins was the first Minnesota high school basketball player to score more than 1,000 points in his prep career.

After three years in the navy, Haskins enrolled at Hamline in 1946. Haskins and future NBA star Vern Mikkelsen helped Hamline with the NAIB national tournament in 1949.

The Lights played their first game on November 1, 1950. They defeated Louisville, 60–48, before a crowd of 2,775 at the St. Paul Auditorium. Haskins and Stan Miasek led the Lights with 11 points. Schultz contributed 6 points.

But within a month, the *Minneapolis Tribune* reported that the Lights were experiencing financial problems. In its December 5 edition, the *Tribune* reported that the Lights were including professional wrestling matches on the same program with the Lights to draw more fans.

On December 15, Louisville defeated the Lights, 81–71, before 1,109 fans at the St. Paul Auditorium. The loss ended the Lights' 8-game home winning streak.

On the same day, according to an Associated Press report, the NBA rejected an application for a franchise from the Lights. NBA president Maurice Podoloff said the bid had been made by Richard K. Headley, the Lights' president and general manager.

On December 19, the Lights defeated Waterloo, 76–70, before 972 fans at the auditorium. The victory, which improved their record to 12-8, came in the Lights' final game.

Two days later, the team folded. Headley told the *Minneapolis Tribune* that the decision was made following a "combination of factors. We dropped a bundle of cash, but if we could have seen something bright in the future we would have stayed in business. But with the [Korean] war conditions, we didn't see a sense of continuing."

Only three of the league's eight teams—Anderson, Sheboygan and Waterloo—were able to play a full schedule. In addition to the Lights, Grand Rapids, Kansas City and Louisville also disbanded. The Denver team relocated to Evansville during the season. The league folded after the season.

Schultz was assigned to Denver, and Haskins was assigned to Waterloo by the league. Haskins didn't report to Waterloo because he was recalled by the navy.

At the end of his service time, he returned to Minnesota and became a high school basketball coach and teacher. He worked for the St. Paul school system for nearly thirty years. He passed away in June 2003 at the age of seventy-eight.

Schultz played two seasons for the Minneapolis Lakers and was a member of the NBA championship teams in 1952 and 1953. He retired as a player in 1953. At the time of his retirement, Schultz and Gene Conley were the only players who had qualified for MLB and NBA pensions.

After his playing career, Schultz coached basketball at St. Paul Mechanic Arts High School and then at Hamline for seven seasons. He died on October 30, 2009, at the age of eighty-seven.

7

THE MINNEAPOLIS LAKERS' IMPACT ON THE NBA

The Minneapolis Lakers were an immediate success on the basketball court after the team was formed in 1947. They won a league title in their first season and went on to win six titles in their first seven years of existence.

They've been called the National Basketball Association's first dynasty. With future Naismith Basketball Hall of Famers George Mikan and Jim Pollard in their lineup, the Lakers became one of the best draws in the NBA.

In their first season, the Lakers were a part of two games that impacted professional basketball's road to diversity. The first was in February 1948, when the Lakers took a break from their National Basketball League (NBL) schedule to play an exhibition against the Harlem Globetrotters in Chicago. On February 19, 1948, in a game played before a crowd of 17,823 at Chicago Stadium, the Globetrotters edged the Lakers, 61–59, on a shot at the buzzer by Ermer Robinson. Mikan led the Lakers with 24 points.

The Lakers went on to finish in first place in the West Division of the NBL. In the first round of the playoffs, the Lakers defeated Oshkosh, 3 games to 1, and then defeated Tri-Cities, 2 games to 0, to advance to the NBL finals. But before the Lakers faced the Rochester Royals in the league's championship series, they took another break in Chicago.

The Lakers, whose playoff series against Tri-Cities ended on March 31, accepted an invitation to play in the tenth annual World Pro Basketball Tournament. The four-day tournament was scheduled for April 8–11.

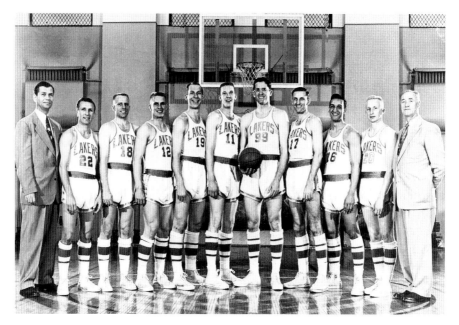

The Minneapolis Lakers, coached by John Kundla (*far left*) and with center George Mikan (*99*), were the NBA's first dynasty. *National Basketball Association.*

Delaying the league finals was criticized in Rochester, New York. Elliot Cushing wrote in the April 5 edition of the *Rochester Democrat and Chronicle*: "Once again, the NBL championship playoff finals are relegated to the background by a pseudo-world tournament in Chicago. This is made possible only because [NBL commissioner] Ward Lambert regards the synthetic Chicago affair more important than the deciding of the championship of his own league. Otherwise he would have ordered Minneapolis to withdraw from the pointless tournament and proceed with the NBL title play."

Cushing went on to write, "In this particular case, however, the postponement works to the Royals advantage."

The Royals, who had finished off their semifinal series against Anderson on April 3, had two starters who were injured, Arnie Risen and Red Holzman.

Lakers general manager Max Winter told the *Minneapolis Tribune* on the eve of the tournament in Chicago that he was surprised Rochester, which had turned down an invitation to play in the tournament, didn't object to the Lakers playing in it. "I wondered why [Royals owner] Les Harrison suddenly changed his attitude and allowed us to play in the Chicago tournament," Winter said. "I wanted to start the final series right away but he stalled off and said he would rather wait until the Chicago tournament was over.

"I asked him, kiddingly, who was hurt, but he said no one was hurt. I thought it was Bill ["Red"] Holzman, who has a bad knee. But now it turns out to be [Royals center] Arnold Risen."

Risen had suffered a broken jaw while closely guarding former Hamline star Howie Schultz in the deciding game of the Anderson series. Risen would not play against the Lakers.

On April 8 in Chicago, the Lakers defeated Wilkes-Barre, the Eastern Pro champion, 98–48, in the first round of the tournament. The next night, the Lakers defeated NBL rival Anderson—one of five NBL teams in the tournament—to advance to the finals.

In the finals, the Lakers faced the New York Rens. The Rens, an independent Black team, had won the tournament in its second year in 1940.

With George Mikan scoring 40 points, the Lakers outlasted the Rens, 75–71, in front of a crowd of 16,892 at Chicago Stadium.

Two days later, the Lakers resumed their bid for the NBL title. The first 2 games of the best-of-5 series with Rochester were played in Minneapolis. The Lakers won, 80–72, on April 13 and 82–67 the next night.

After a travel day on April 15, the series shifted to Rochester on April 16. The Royals avoided a sweep by winning Game 3, 74–60, before the Lakers closed out the series with a 75–65 victory on April 17.

Mikan scored 110 points in the 4 games against Rochester. The league championship game completed a stretch where the Lakers had won 38 of 47 games. They went 27-7 over their final 34 regular-season games—including 11 consecutive games in one stretch—to finish the regular season with a 43-17 record. In the postseason, they went 8-2 in the NBL playoffs and 3-0 at the World Tournament.

While the Lakers' NBL championship—in their first season in the league—brought them accolades, author John Christgau wrote in his book *Tricksters in the Madhouse* that the 1948 Lakers/Globetrotters game "represented an important step toward [racial] equality."

Author Ben Green, in his history of the Globetrotters, *Spinning the Globe: The Rise, Fall and Return to Greatness of the Harlem Globetrotters*, called the meeting between the Lakers and the Globetrotters in February 1948 "one of the most memorable basketball games of all time."

According to a history of the Harlem Globetrotters on the team's website, "In 1948 and 1949, the Globetrotters stunned the world by twice defeating the World Champion Minneapolis Lakers of the NBA. The victories over the Lakers accelerated the integration of the NBA, as Globetrotter Nathaniel 'Sweetwater' Clifton became the first African-

American player to sign an NBA contract when he joined the famed New York Knicks in 1950."

After the 1948 and 1949 games between the Globetrotters and Lakers, the teams played 5 more exhibitions over the next three years. The Lakers won all 5 games. After their game in January 1952, the teams met one more time, in January 1958. The Lakers won the game.

During the 1948–49 season, the Rens joined the NBL after the Detroit franchise folded after 19 games. The Rens played out of Dayton, Ohio, and became the first all-Black team in a professional basketball league.

After the 1947–48 season, the Lakers left the NBL and joined the Basketball Association of America (BAA). In 1949, the NBL and BAA merged to form the NBA. A Minnesota native played an instrumental role in the merger.

Fred Zollner, the owner of the Fort Wayne (Indiana) Zollner Pistons, convinced the other league owners to merge. The owners agreed with Zollner because he had helped the NBL survive lean years during World War II.

According to a story in the December 18, 1967 issue of *Sports Illustrated*, Zollner, who was born in Little Falls, Minnesota, and grew up in Duluth before earning a degree in mechanical engineering from the University of Minnesota, "helped keep it [NBL] afloat by lending it large sums, while many clubs failed to pay their dues."

At the 1975 Silver Anniversary All-Star Game, played in Phoenix, Zollner was named "Mr. Pro Basketball" in recognition of his efforts to support the NBA. Zollner, who owned the Pistons until 1974 (they moved from Fort Wayne to Detroit in 1957), was inducted into the Naismith Basketball Hall of Fame in 1999. He died in January 1985 at the age of eighty-one.

8

JOHN WOODEN

A MISSED CONNECTION

After UCLA defeated Louisville, 75–74, in the semifinals of the NCAA men's basketball Final Four on March 29, 1975, in San Diego, California, UCLA coach John Wooden announced his retirement.

Two days later, UCLA defeated Kentucky, 92–85, for the national championship. The Bruins' tenth national title in the last twelve seasons cemented Wooden's legacy as one of the greatest college basketball coaches of all time.

About a week after the championship game, renowned sportswriter Red Smith of the *New York Times* wrote in a nationally syndicated column that Wooden's legendary twenty-seven-year career at UCLA almost didn't happen.

Smith wrote: "As the Indiana State coach in 1948, he [Wooden] was being sought by both UCLA and Minnesota when a blizzard prevented Minnesota officials with an offer he probably would have accepted. Having not heard from Minnesota by the appointed hour, he accepted the UCLA job."

In his autobiography *They Call Me Coach*, published in 1988, Wooden said a time was set for a phone call with each school to discuss his decision. Wooden wrote: "As it was set up, [University of Minnesota athletic director] Frank McCormick was to call me for my answer at 6 p.m. and [UCLA athletic director] Wilbur Johns would call at 7 [p.m.]. There was a snowstorm raging in Minneapolis that day and Frank got snowed in and couldn't get to a phone on time. I didn't know of any problem so when Mr. Johns called, right on time, I accepted the UCLA job. When McCormick finally reached

Coach
Frank
McCormick

Left, top: Frank McCormick served as the baseball coach and athletic director at the University of Minnesota in the 1930s and 1940s. *University of Minnesota.*

Left, bottom: Frank McCormick, who served as the University of Minnesota athletic director from 1932 to 1941 and from 1945 to 1950, nearly hired John Wooden as the university's basketball coach in 1948. *University of Minnesota.*

Opposite: Frank McCormick, a member of the American Baseball Coaches Association Hall of Fame, led the University of Minnesota baseball team from 1930 to 1941. *University of Minnesota.*

me about an hour later, he told me everything was 'all set.' It's too late, I told him, I have already accepted the job at UCLA."

Over the years, some details of the story have changed. In *Wooden: A Coach's Life*, written by Seth Davis and published in 2015, the story was that a spring snowstorm (on April 17) had knocked down telephone lines in Minneapolis and that McCormick was unable to call at the prearranged time.

Wooden told *Minneapolis Tribune* columnist Sid Hartman in 1964 that he "leaned towards" the Minnesota job because he had played basketball at Purdue in the Big Ten Conference.

While much of the story about the University of Minnesota missing out on the chance to hire Wooden is true, some of the facts are in dispute. Blaming the missed connection on a blizzard in Minneapolis is easiest to refute.

On March 2, 1948, a day after the Gophers defeated Wisconsin in Minneapolis in their season finale, Gophers basketball coach Dave MacMillan announced his retirement. The 1947–48 season was MacMillan's eighteenth as the Gophers' coach. On March 3, McCormick told reporters, "I have no idea who the new coach will be and don't know when I will be ready to make a recommendation to the [University of Minnesota] president."

Wooden, who had been a three-time All-American as a player at Purdue, was in his second season as the Indiana State basketball coach. The Sycamores had advanced to the NAIB national tournament in Kansas City, Missouri. The thirty-two-team tournament began on March 9.

Indiana State defeated Hamline of St. Paul, Minnesota, 66–65, in the semifinals on March 12 to advance to the championship game. On March 13, Indiana State lost to Louisville, 82–70. The Sycamores finished the season with a 27-7 record.

On his return to Terre Haute, Wooden, who was also Indiana State's baseball coach, started preparing his team for its season opener on April 9.

For much of March, Wooden was busy with baseball practice and banquets. On March 19, he spoke at a banquet at the Indiana High School Basketball Tournament. On March 24, he was initiated as an Elks member in Terre Haute. That date is significant, because the National Association of Basketball Coaches (NABC) annual convention began that day in New York City. There has been some speculation that the convention is where Wooden made his first contact with Minnesota and UCLA about their vacant coaching positions, but he was not in attendance.

On April 2, Wooden spoke at a banquet in Clinton, Indiana. A week later, the Sycamores baseball team opened its season with an 8–7 victory over Eastern Illinois in Charleston, Illinois.

After the opener, Wooden traveled to Los Angeles to meet with UCLA officials. The *Los Angeles Times* reported in its April 13 edition that Wooden "was closeted yesterday" with UCLA athletic director Wilbur Johns. The UCLA position was open because Johns had stepped down from coaching to concentrate on his athletic director duties.

April 13 was also the day that Wooden was mentioned in Minneapolis newspapers for the first time as a candidate for the Minnesota job. The *Minneapolis Tribune* reported that Wooden and McCormick would meet in Chicago on the upcoming weekend, as McCormick was traveling to New York City for a U.S. Olympic Committee meeting scheduled for April 17 and 18.

It is not known when Wooden and McCormick had their meeting in Chicago. The Sycamores baseball team played a home game against Anderson on April 16 and a doubleheader at Valparaiso on April 17. The April 16 game was scheduled for 3:00 p.m., so Wooden and McCormick could have met in Chicago either late on April 15 or early on April 16 to give Wooden time to make the 180-mile trip back to Terre Haute in time for the Anderson game. In an interview years later, Wooden said that after the meeting in Chicago, McCormick promised to call in one week.

Wooden said on several occasions that April 17 was the day that he was supposed to be called by Johns and McCormick.

On April 17, the Sycamores baseball team made the 167-mile trip from Terre Haute to Valparaiso, Indiana, for a doubleheader scheduled to start at 1:30 p.m. Valparaiso won the pair of seven-inning games, 7–0 and 5–3. The doubleheader was likely over around 6:00 p.m., so Wooden wouldn't have been home for the phone calls. It's more likely that the calls were arranged for Sunday, April 18.

By Sunday evening, the Olympic Committee meeting in New York was probably completed. McCormick was back in Minneapolis on April 19, so depending on his mode of travel (plane or train), McCormick could have still been in New York.

A check of the weather for Minneapolis, New York and Terre Haute on April 18 shows a nice spring day in each locale. New York City was sunny with a high near sixty degrees, Minneapolis was partly cloudy with a high around sixty-five and Terre Haute was partly cloudy and mild.

Over the years, the stories about a "blizzard" delaying the Minnesota phone call to Wooden have centered on McCormick. He had grown up in Wagner, South Dakota—about 110 miles southwest of Sioux Falls, South Dakota—and still had business interests in the area. He occasionally visited

Ozzie Cowles was named the Minnesota Gophers' men's basketball coach after John Wooden accepted the UCLA job over the Minnesota offer. *University of Minnesota.*

there on weekends. It's been suggested that the date of the phone call is incorrect and that it was scheduled for early April.

A snowstorm did hit parts of South Dakota and North Dakota on April 7, but the storm missed the Sioux Falls area. An earlier winter storm on March 26 had knocked down telephone lines in northern Minnesota, but McCormick was in New York that weekend.

In addition to the blizzard story, Wooden mentioned in several interviews over the years that he was offered the Minnesota job by McCormick but that he and McCormick "disagreed because the University wanted the new coach to retain MacMillan as an assistant [coach]."

MacMillan was going to be paid for the final year of his contract. Wooden said he wanted to bring his assistant from Indiana State, Ed Powell, and that McCormick told him that the school president, James Morrill, and the board of regents would have to approve it. In its April 20 edition, the morning *Minneapolis Tribune* reported that McCormick had returned to Minneapolis on April 19 and told the newspaper he "would have no announcement until the Board of Regents approved the choice."

Wooden was announced as the UCLA coach on April 20. The news appeared in the April 20 edition of the afternoon *Minneapolis Star.*

On May 14, the University of Minnesota named Minnesota native Ozzie Cowles to replace MacMillan. Cowles, who had coached the University of Michigan to the Big Ten title in the 1947–48 season, went on to coach the Gophers through 1959.

McCormick retired as the Gophers' athletic director in 1950. He moved to Los Angeles, where he became the supervisor of basketball officials for the Pacific Coast Conference, of which UCLA was a member. McCormick died in Orange County, California, in 1976 at the age of eighty-one. Wooden died in 2010 at the age of ninety-nine.

A little over two years after the university missed out on hiring Wooden, athletic director Ike Armstrong, who replaced McCormick, offered the vacant Gopher football coaching position—Bernie Bierman had retired following the 1950 season—to two future coaching legends: Bear Bryant and Bud Wilkinson. A snowstorm might have affected the decision by one of them to not accept the job offer.

Wilkinson, a Minneapolis native and former Gopher star from the 1930s who was coaching the University of Oklahoma football team, announced in early December 1950 that he could not accept the Gophers' offer because he still had three years remaining on his contract at Oklahoma.

Soon after that announcement, Bryant was offered the job and visited Minneapolis. Reportedly, Bryant was unhappy with his situation at Kentucky, where he had coached since 1946. But he declined the offer.

In January 1951, the Gophers hired former Ohio State coach Wes Fesler.

About twenty-five years later, Bryant returned to Minneapolis for a coaching clinic. He told longtime *Minneapolis Tribune* columnist Dick Cullum: "When I arrived here that December the weather was perfect, bright and warm. We had a pleasant interview. But when I woke up the next day the ground was covered with 18 inches of snow. I'm a southern boy and I got out of there as fast as I could. I don't know if they wanted me, but I think they got my message."

Cullum wrote that he had heard another version about Bryant's visit to Minneapolis: "Minnesota wanted Bryant, but Bryant had apparently told his close friends that he felt he couldn't win at Minnesota." Minnesota at the time did not offer athletic scholarships.

According to the December 7, 1950 issue of the afternoon *Minneapolis Star*, Minneapolis had received "five inches of new snow today to bring the depth on the ground to 16 inches. The weather bureau has recorded 14 inches thus far in December."

So, perhaps a snowstorm did play a role. Coincidentally, several weeks later, on January 1, 1951, Bryant's Kentucky Wildcats defeated Wilkinson's Oklahoma Sooners, 13–7, in the Sugar Bowl in New Orleans. The loss ended Oklahoma's 31-game winning streak.

9

JEANNE ARTH

A TENNIS GIANT FROM ST. PAUL

Tennis has been played at the All England Club in London since 1876. The club's annual tournament, Wimbledon, was held for the first time in 1877 and is the world's oldest tennis tournament.

Within a decade of that first tournament, tennis arrived in Minnesota. In the late 1880s, the sport was being played at half a dozen sites in the Twin Cities: Hamline Turf Club, White Bear Yacht Club, Town and Country Club and Ashland Courts in St. Paul and the Minikahda Club and Hotel Lafayette/St. Louis in Minneapolis.

The first Minnesotan to be ranked nationally in tennis was George Belden of Minneapolis. In 1898, Belden, considered the champion of the Northwest, was ranked No. 10. In 1913, Gwendolyn Rees of St. Paul became the first women's champion of the Northwest and the first woman from Minnesota to be ranked nationally, when she was ranked No. 10.

Despite the long history of the sport in Minnesota, it took eighty-two years before a Minnesotan competed at Wimbledon. In 1959, Jeanne Arth, a high school teacher from St. Paul, became the first Minnesotan to play tennis internationally when she competed at the French Open and Wimbledon, despite playing tennis just four months a year.

In a story about Arth in 2002, the *Minneapolis Star Tribune* reported, "A giant of the tennis world lives in St. Paul and hardly anyone knows it."

Arth, who was born in St. Paul in 1935, started playing tennis at a young age. She and her sister Shirley, who was two years older, started practicing at the St. Paul Tennis Club, which was near their home. "A lot of wealthy people belonged there," Arth told the *Star Tribune* in 2002, "but we didn't have any money so we never became members. The caretaker used to see my sister and I walking to the playground down the street to hit tennis balls, so he said we could use the club's courts if we came before the women started practicing in the morning."

Eventually, the Arth sisters were able to play at the club.

"When I was about 9 or 10," Arth said, "the women would let us fill in if someone didn't show up. Then we started to play doubles against them."

The Arth sisters, who also played basketball and softball, developed into a good doubles team. The sisters began playing in Northwest Lawn Tennis Association (now USTA Northern Section) tournaments when Jeanne was eleven years old.

Jeanne Arth was the first Minnesotan to play at Wimbledon. *St. Catherine University*.

In August 1948, Jeanne, who was thirteen at the time, and Shirley teamed to win the doubles title at the River Forest (Illinois) Invitational. Jeanne also won the singles title. In late August, the pair competed in the National Amateur meet in Philadelphia. Both reached the third round in singles, and in doubles they reached the quarterfinals. At the end of the year, the sisters were ranked third nationally in junior girls doubles by the U.S. Lawn Tennis Association.

After graduating from St. Paul Central High School, Jeanne enrolled at the College of St. Catherine (now St. Catherine University) in St. Paul. In September 1953, she reached the finals of the National Amateur Tournament in Forest Hills, New York, where she was defeated by Wimbledon champion Maureen Connolly in straight sets. It was the third straight year Connolly had won the National Amateur title.

In June 1954, Arth was one of fourteen participants in the first national college girls' tennis tournament. Arth reached the finals of the tournament, which was hosted by Washington University in St. Louis.

Arth reached the tournament's singles final in 1955 and 1956 and teamed with a different partner each year to win the tournament's doubles championship in each of her three times competing at the tournament.

After graduating from St. Catherine in 1956, Arth began her teaching career while continuing to play tennis. In the summer of 1957, she began playing in national women's tournaments on clay and grass. Despite playing tennis competitively just four months out of the year and competing against many players who played year-round, Arth reached No. 7 in singles and No. 3 (with Pat Naud of California) in doubles in U.S. women's rankings.

In 1958, Arth and partner Darlene Hard of California teamed to win the U.S. Women's Doubles championship in Chestnut Hill, Massachusetts. In the championship match, Arth and Hard, who were unseeded, defeated top-seeded Althea Gibson and Maria Bueno, the reigning Wimbledon Ladies' Doubles champion, in three sets. Gibson was ranked No. 1, and Bueno was ranked No. 2 in the U.S. women's singles rankings.

A week later at the U.S. Open in Forest Hills, Arth and Hard each reached the semifinals of the U.S. Singles championship. Hard defeated Arth, 7–5, 6–2.

After the tournament, Arth returned home to Minnesota and her teaching career at Holy Angels Academy in Richfield. She told the *Minneapolis Tribune* that despite her successful year, she wasn't going to give up teaching to play tennis full time. "Professional tennis opportunities for women are too limited," Arth said. "What can you do—play a few matches, or maybe get a club teaching job? I'd rather teach school. I can hardly wait to get back to it."

At the end of 1958, Arth was ranked No. 6 in the national singles rankings and No. 1 in doubles.

In 1959, Arth and Hard received invitations to play at Wimbledon. Prior to 1968, only top-ranked amateur players competed at Wimbledon by invitation. Arth credited the Northwest Lawn Tennis Association for helping her make the trip to England. "When I was playing, there was no money," she told the *Minneapolis Star Tribune* in 1986, "The Northwest Tennis patrons helped pay my expenses. Without them I wouldn't have been able to do it."

To prepare for Wimbledon, Arth was able to play in several tournaments. In May, she reached the third round in both singles and doubles (with partner Marta Peterdy) at the French Open in Paris. In June, Arth reached the singles semifinals of the Kent Lawn Tennis tournament in Beckenham, England. Arth and Hard reached the finals of the London Club Tournament.

At Wimbledon, Arth lost to Rosie Reyes, 6–1, 6–4 in the second round of singles.

In mixed doubles, Arth teamed with Australian Bob Mark to reach the second round, while Hard and Australian Rod Laver teamed to win the title.

Arth and Hard were the top seed in doubles. They were nearly perfect in winning their first four matches: 6–1, 6–1 in the first round; 6–2, 6–0 in the second round; 6–0, 6–1 in the quarterfinals; and 6–0, 6–2 in the semifinals.

In the championship match on Centre Court, Arth and Hard rallied after losing the first set to American Beverly Fleitz and England's Christine Truman. Arth and Hard won, 2–6, 6–2, 6–3.

"Ask any tennis player in the world which one court they'd like to play on and they'll say 'Centre Court, Wimbledon.' Rod Laver once described Wimbledon as the cathedral of tennis, and Centre Court is the high altar," Arth told the *Minneapolis Star Tribune* in 2002. "There's so much history there, and I was lucky enough to play five or six times at Centre Court."

After returning to the United States, Arth and Hard teamed up to help the United States defeat Great Britain in the Wightman Cup. Arth and Hard won their doubles match, and Hard went 1-1 in singles as the U.S. defeated Great Britain, 4-3, in Sewickley, Pennsylvania.

Two weeks later, Arth and Hard defended their doubles title at the U.S. Open.

In the fall of 1959, Arth ended her competition on the women's tennis circuit. "I knew if I wanted to get better," Arth said in the 2002 interview with the *Star Tribune*, "I'd have to give up my teaching career and move someplace where I could play all year. I didn't want to give up teaching. I enjoyed it and knew I couldn't make a living playing tennis anyway."

Arth continued playing in USTA/Northern Section events. In the section's rankings, Arth was ranked No. 1 in singles each year from 1951 to 1969 and No. 1 in doubles each year from 1949 to 1969.

In July 1971, after winning the section mixed doubles title, Arth announced she would be playing in the upcoming U.S. Open. She emphasized that her first appearance at the U.S. Open since 1959 was not the beginning of a comeback. "I am going to the nationals with Gussie [Moran] just for fun," Arth told the *Minneapolis Star*.

In singles, Arth lost to Billie Jean King in straight sets. "She's just too good, I'm just too old," Arth said after the match. King went on to win the tournament singles title.

In women's doubles, Arth and Moran lost in the first round. In mixed doubles, Arth and Ham Richardson lost in the first round to King and Owen Davidson, who went on to win the title.

Arth was a physical education teacher from 1956 to 1976 and then a high school guidance counselor from 1976 to 1993.

She is a member of four Halls of Fame—Minnesota Tennis, Minnesota Sports, University of St. Catherine and Intercollegiate Tennis Association—

because of her accomplishments as a tennis player. But she told the *Minneapolis Star Tribune* in 2002: "I've had a very satisfying life. Tennis was incidental. I did well when I played, but it certainly didn't dominate my life. You just can't think about 'if this had happened, or that, or what if I'd live in California and could play year round.' I've had a happy good life."

Arth's favorite tennis memory? Teaming with Hard to beat Gibson and Bueno at the 1958 U.S. Open. "It was my biggest thrill ever," she said. "It was so unexpected and they were so good."

After Arth played at Wimbledon, it was thirty-five years before another woman from Minnesota played at Wimbledon. Ginger Helgeson, who was born in St. Cloud and raised in Edina, played at Wimbledon for the first time in 1994. In 2008, Rochester native Bethanie Mattek-Sands competed at Wimbledon for the first time.

10

SPENCE HARRIS

A MAJOR STAR IN THE MINOR LEAGUES

In August 1959—two weeks past his fifty-ninth birthday—Anthony Spencer "Spence" Harris played in an old-timers baseball game at Metropolitan Stadium.

In his only at bat of the game, which featured former Minneapolis Millers and St. Paul Saints players, Harris hit a double to center. Gene Mauch, the manager of the Minneapolis Millers, marveled at Harris's hitting ability.

Mauch told Halsey Hall of the *Minneapolis Star* that he was struck by "the beautiful ease with which Spencer Harris got his double."

That ability was a constant for Harris during a twenty-eight-year professional baseball career. Harris, who spent parts of four seasons in the major leagues, played for the Minneapolis Millers from 1928 to 1937. In his ten seasons with the Millers, he never hit below .300.

After the decade with the Millers, he played eight seasons in the Triple-A Pacific Coast League. At the age of forty-eight, in his final season as a player, he batted .338 in a combined 45 games for two minor-league teams.

Harris amassed career totals for his minor-league career that are unlikely to be topped. According to research by the Society for American Baseball Research (SABR), there have more than 310,000 players in the history of minor-league baseball. Harris's career totals of 3,617 hits, 2,287 runs scored, 743 doubles and 5,434 total bases are the most in minor-league history. Harris is fourth on the minor-league career RBIs list with 1,769. The top two players on the list, Nick Cullop (1,857 RBIs) and Buzz Arlett (1,786 RBIs), also played for the Millers. Cullop and Harris were Millers teammates in 1930, and Arlett and Harris were teammates in 1934, 1935 and 1936. Jim Poole is third on the career RBIs list (1,785).

Including the 94 hits he had in 164 major-league games, Harris had 3,711 hits during his professional career. Of the more than 20,200 players who have appeared in a major-league game through the 2022 season, only 4— Pete Rose (4,256), Ty Cobb (4,189), Hank Aaron (3,771) and Stan Musial (3,630)—collected more career hits than Harris's minor-league total.

Harris, who was born in Duluth and attended high school in Seattle, Washington, made his professional debut in June 1921 for the Tacoma Tigers of the Pacific International League. Harris, who was two months shy of his twenty-first birthday, hit a home run in his first professional game.

After hitting .271 for the Tigers in his rookie season, his contract was purchased by the Philadelphia Athletics of the American League.

In 1922, he played for Bay City in the Class B Michigan-Ontario League. He batted .340 in 121 games to earn a promotion to the Athletics in September. But after suffering a sprained ankle, he didn't appear in a game for the A's.

He began the 1923 season with Shreveport of the Texas League. After hitting .243 in 12 games, he was sent back to Bay City. Over the rest of the season, he batted .284 in 125 games as the Wolves won the league title with an 80-51 record.

Harris returned to Bay City in 1924 and was instrumental in the Wolves winning another league title. He batted .319 with 7 home runs, 68 RBIs and 35 stolen bases for the team, which went 86-50.

After the season, his contract was purchased by the Chicago White Sox of the American League, and he spent the 1925 and 1926 seasons with the White Sox. In 1925, he batted .283 in 56 games; he hit .252 in 80 games in 1926. The White Sox sent Harris back to the minors for the 1927 season.

He had an outstanding season for Shreveport in 1927, batting .354 with 201 hits, 12 home runs and 89 RBIs. He led the Texas League with 60 doubles.

In January 1928, the Minneapolis Millers purchased Harris's contract for $10,000. Charles Johnson wrote in the *Minneapolis Star* that Harris was "a colorful young player" who had "impressed everyone with his speed on the bases and in the outfield. He bats left-handed and is a good socker, according to averages and reports."

Except for two brief stints—6 games with the Washington Senators in 1929 and 22 games with the Philadelphia Athletics in 1930—the five-foot, nine-inch, 145-pound Harris was a mainstay in the Millers' lineup for the next ten seasons.

Harris was an immediate hit in 1928 in his first season with the Millers. He batted .327 with 219 hits and 127 RBIs while leading the American Association in runs scored (133), doubles (41) and home runs (32).

In the five seasons between 1929 and 1933, Harris batted .340, .363, .341, .352 and .355, respectively, for the Millers. In 1932, the Millers won 100 games on their way to the American Association title. The team lost to the International League champion Newark Bears in the Junior World Series.

In 1937, his tenth and final season with the Millers, he batted .326. A week after the end of the season, a group of major-league players competed in an exhibition game at Nicollet Park, the Millers' home field. Harris hit a triple off future Hall of Famer Bob Feller.

In December 1937, at Organized Baseball's annual winter meetings, the Boston Red Sox of the American League announced they had acquired outfielder Ted Williams from San Diego of the Pacific Coast League in exchange for two players and cash. One of the players sent by Boston to San Diego in the deal for the nineteen-year-old future Hall of Famer was Harris. The Millers had become a Red Sox farm team in 1936.

Veteran Minneapolis sportswriter Halsey Hall wrote in the *Minneapolis Journal* that Williams was "one of the greatest hitting prospects to ever come along." Hall was prophetic. In 1938—his only season with the Millers—Williams won the American Association Triple Crown with a .366 batting average, 43 home runs and 142 RBI.

Harris batted .301 with 7 home runs and 92 RBIS in 1938 with San Diego. He spent seven more seasons in the Pacific Coast League. Beginning in 1946, he spent the next two and a half seasons with Yakima (Washington) of the Class B Western International League. In the final month of the 1948 season, he was a player-manager for Marysville (California) of the Class D Far West League.

During his nearly three-decade minor-league career, Harris batted over .300 in seventeen seasons and finished with a career average of .318. He had more than 200 hits in a season five times—his career-high was 224 with the Millers in 1933—and drove in more than 100 runs six times.

When SABR picked fifteen players for its all-time minor-league All-Stars, Harris was one of them.

After his playing career ended, he briefly managed in the minor leagues and scouted for the New York Mets. Harris lived in Minneapolis after his playing career. He worked at Juster's, a clothing store in downtown Minneapolis. He played golf regularly until he was in his late seventies. He died on July 3, 1982, in Minneapolis at the age of eighty-one.

In August 1950, Harris was asked by the *Seattle Times* how he had continued to have success as a hitter past the age of forty. He replied: "Eyes and wrists. As long as they don't go…I'll be able to hit the ball when I'm 60 years old."

11

PRO FOOTBALL COMES
TO MINNESOTA

By early 1959, efforts to lure a professional football team to the Twin
Cities, either by relocation or expansion, had stalled.

The situation dramatically changed in the summer of 1959,
and within eight months, the Twin Cities had accepted franchises in two
professional football leagues.

The announcement by the National Football League in January
1960 that Minnesota and Dallas had been awarded expansion teams
completed a whirlwind three months, which saw Minnesota go from
being a charter member of a new league in November to joining the
established NFL in January. Minnesota's flirtation with the fledgling
league has been largely forgotten.

The flurry of activity in late 1959 had been preceded by several
frustrating years for the Twin Cities, which saw a bid by a group of
Minnesota businessmen to purchase the NFL's Chicago Cardinals
franchise turned down and efforts to convince NFL commissioner Bert
Bell that his twelve-team league should expand. Bell repeatedly said
expansion for his league was too risky financially.

What changed in the summer of 1959 was that the reluctance of the
NFL to expand got the attention of the United States Senate. Led by
the efforts of Senator Estes Kefauver of Tennessee, the Senate began
hearings in July 1959 about the monopolies of the NFL and other
professional sports leagues.

Max Winter was instrumental in bringing the Minneapolis Lakers and the Minnesota Vikings to the Twin Cities. *Minnesota Vikings.*

On July 28, 1959, Bell revealed to a U.S. Senate subcommittee hearing that the NFL, which had last expanded in 1950, would expand by four teams within the next three years. Bell also disclosed that a second professional football league was being formed and would begin play in 1960.

Bell said the new league would have eight teams and mentioned that the Minneapolis–St. Paul region would have one of the franchises.

The new league was the brainchild of Texas oil tycoon Lamar Hunt, who was the son of H.L. Hunt, one of the richest people in the United States at that time. Lamar Hunt began considering forming his own league after being turned down in his bid to buy the Chicago Cardinals in November 1958. While Hunt was negotiating the purchase, the Cardinals' owners had turned down an offer by Minnesotan Max Winter. After being turned down, Hunt approached Bell about acquiring an expansion team and was again rebuffed.

In June 1959, Hunt met with a group from the Twin Cities: William Boyer, H.P. Skoglund and Winter. The group committed to Hunt's new league.

Three days after Bell's testimony in July 1959, the name of Hunt's new league and six of the franchises were announced. The American Football League (AFL) said it would field teams in Dallas, Denver, Houston, Los Angeles, Minneapolis–St. Paul and New York City and would add two more teams from a group that included Buffalo, Kansas City, Miami, San Francisco and Seattle.

The unveiling of the AFL got the attention of the NFL. In late August, owner and coach of the Chicago Bears and chairman of the NFL's expansion committee George Halas announced that the NFL would expand to Dallas and Houston for the 1960 season. Halas said the NFL was considering additional expansion for the 1961 season with the cities of Boston, Buffalo, Denver, Louisville, Miami, Minneapolis–St. Paul and New Orleans under consideration.

Two events after that announcement by Halas brought dramatic change. On October 11, Bell, who had led the league since 1946, suffered a heart attack while attending a game in Philadelphia and died suddenly at the age of sixty-five. NFL officials soon learned that the league wouldn't be able to field an expansion team in Houston in 1960 because of stadium issues.

The NFL began a campaign behind the scenes to lure AFL owners to join the NFL.

In late November 1959, AFL officials gathered at the Pick Nicollet Hotel in downtown Minneapolis for the league's first player draft. Representatives from the six charter franchises were joined by the league's seventh and eighth franchises, Boston and Buffalo.

That same weekend, the NFL's Chicago Cardinals played their second "home" game of the season at Metropolitan Stadium in Bloomington. On Sunday, November 22, a crowd of 26,625 saw the New York Giants defeat the Cardinals, 30–20. A month earlier, on October 25, 20,112 spectators saw the Philadelphia Eagles, whose quarterback was future Minnesota Vikings coach Norm Van Brocklin, defeat the Cardinals, 28–24.

Hunt and Winter rode together for the eleven-mile trip from downtown Minneapolis to suburban Bloomington for the Cardinals/Giants game, which was scheduled to begin at 1:05 p.m. Years later, Hunt told a Kansas City reporter that during the ride, Winter mentioned that he had received a phone call from Halas. Halas told Winter that the NFL would admit four of the AFL franchises and that ten of twelve NFL teams had approved Minnesota's application, which had been made in August, for an NFL team. Hunt and Winter agreed that the offer would be discussed after the game.

A six-hour organizational meeting between AFL owners followed the Cardinals/Giants game on Sunday. At some point that day, Halas wired Max Winter, the head of the Minnesota group, that ten NFL teams had approved Minnesota's application. The application had been made in August. Winter walked out of the meeting before the meeting finished.

A headline in the Monday issue of the *Minneapolis Tribune* read, "Twin Cities May Get National Grid Team." Hunt told the *Tribune*, "Twin Cities representatives have told me they have no intentions of withdrawing from the American league."

When the AFL conducted its first draft on Monday, November 23, H.P. Skoglund was the lone representative of the Minnesota group. The Minnesota team made University of Wisconsin defensive back Dale Hackbart its first-round draft choice. Hackbart later played for the Minnesota Vikings from 1966 to 1970.

In January 1960, NFL owners gathered in Miami for their annual meeting. The first order of business was to hire a replacement for Bell. After naming

Pete Rozelle to replace Bell, they voted to expand by two teams: Dallas, which would begin play in 1960; and Minnesota, which would begin in 1961.

The Vikings ownership group consisted of Winter, Bill Boyer, Ole Haugsrud, B.H. Ridder and Skoglund.

Losing the Minnesota franchise created a vacancy for the AFL and its commissioner, Joe Foss, the former governor of South Dakota. On February 1, the league announced that Oakland had been awarded the franchise forfeited by Minnesota. Oakland edged out Atlanta in a vote by the league's owners.

On April 5, the Oakland franchise announced that it would be called the Señors. That name was selected from the ten thousand names submitted by citizens. Ten days later, the team announced that it would instead be called the Raiders. The first players assigned to the Raiders by the AFL were the original fourteen players selected by Minneapolis–St. Paul in the November draft.

Eventually, the Raiders and Minnesota Vikings would meet on the playing field.

The AFL and NFL announced on June 8, 1966, that the rival leagues would merge. For the next four seasons, the leagues maintained separate schedules before officially merging at the start of the 1970 season.

Starting in 1967, the Vikings played preseason games against AFL teams. The Raiders and Vikings met for the first time when they opened the 1973 regular season at Metropolitan Stadium in Bloomington. The Vikings won the game, 24–16.

Following the 1976 season, the Vikings and Raiders met in Super Bowl XI on January 9, 1977, at the Rose Bowl in Pasadena, California. The Raiders defeated the Vikings, 32–14. It was the fourth loss in the Super Bowl in an eight-season span for the Vikings. Through the 2021 season, the Vikings have not made an appearance in a Super Bowl since.

12

OLE HAUGSRUD

A PROMISE KEPT BY THE NFL

Ernie Nevers's Eskimos and Ole Haugsrud helped the National Football League weather a storm in its first decade.

The Eskimos, based in Duluth, Minnesota, and owned by a then twenty-seven-year-old local businessman named Ole Haugsrud, helped the fledgling league survive a financially challenging 1926 season.

The Eskimos, who featured three future members of the Pro Football Hall of Fame—Johnny "Blood" McNally, Walt Kiesling and Nevers—toured the United States, playing 29 games, 13 against NFL teams, in 117 days. In one 8-day stretch, the Eskimos played 5 games.

According to *The Football Encyclopedia* in its recap of the 1926 NFL season, "Nevers gave the NFL a needed heroic image and some gate relief in a season of red ink and rain." Of the league's twenty-two teams, ten folded after that season, but the NFL survived to play its sixth season.

While Nevers and the Eskimos were acknowledged for their roles, it would take more than thirty years for Haugsrud to be rewarded for his contributions and his patience.

The Eskimos had started as an independent pro team called the Kelleys and joined the NFL in 1923. Haugsrud joined the team in 1924 as the manager. After two seasons, the team's owners were ready to fold it. Haugsrud bought the team for one dollar.

In 1929, Haugsrud sold the Eskimos franchise to a group in New Jersey. The sales agreement included a clause that went unpublicized. As part of

Ole Haugsrud owned the Duluth Eskimos of the NFL in the 1920s and had an ownership stake in the Minnesota Vikings. *Minnesota Vikings.*

the agreement, the NFL quietly promised Haugsrud that he would receive a share of the next NFL franchise in Minnesota.

In the ensuing years, Haugsrud worked for the NFL's Chicago Cardinals and scouted for several NFL teams.

When a group of Minnesota businessmen, led by Max Winter, was awarded an NFL expansion team in January 1960 (to begin play in 1961), Haugsrud was offered the opportunity to buy 10 percent of the franchise for $60,000.

Haugsrud, who had attended the NFL's annual league meeting every year since 1922, was rewarded for his patience. He accepted the offer. He served as the Vikings' first board chairman.

In 1965, Haugsrud was presented an award for his lifetime contributions to Minnesota sports. *Minneapolis Tribune* columnist Dick Cullum, who had been a sportswriter in Minneapolis since 1922, wrote that Haugsrud "was a driving force behind Minnesota's obtaining a franchise in 1960. Ole was the only man determined that we would have professional football return to Minnesota some day. When the Vikings franchise was awarded his job was fulfilled."

After Haugsrud died in Duluth in March 1976, Cullum reminisced about him in a column in the March 15, 1976 edition of the *Minneapolis Tribune.* "There could not have been a sweeter man in sports than Ole Haugsrud, who died in Duluth Saturday. Yet, he has been the victim of a cruel injustice. He should have been enshrined in the Pro Football Hall of Fame long ago as one of the foremost contributors to the game; but justice has not been done. When Haugsrud, George Halas and pro football were all young, the National Football league was a feeble, struggling enterprise and in danger."

At the annual league meeting following the 1926 season, Halas praised Haugsrud's signing of Ernie Nevers. Nevers, who was born in Willow River, Minnesota, and attended high school in Superior, Wisconsin, was an All-American football player for Stanford and also played baseball at the major-league level.

According to Cullum, Halas told Haugsrud, "Ole, you have saved the National Football League."

Cullum wrote that the league's decision to expand to Minnesota was "in good measure because Halas cared for Haugsrud. Halas controlled most of the NFL's decisions at the time. He had no loyalty to Minnesota. His loyalty was to Ole. This may have been the single determining factor that created the Minnesota Vikings."

Cullum said Haugsrud played a big role in convincing the Philadelphia Eagles to hold training camp in Grand Rapids, Minnesota, and the New York Giants to train at Gustavus Adolphus College in St. Peter, Minnesota. During the late 1940s and the 1950s, Haugsrud also helped set up an annual exhibition game to be played in the Twin Cities, usually involving the Green Bay Packers.

Cullum finished his column by writing, "One of the reasons—but not the only one—why he belongs in the Football Hall of Fame is that his inclusion would be the ideal reminder that important things are worth doing for their value, not for personal glory."

The headline on the news story in the *Minneapolis Tribune* after Haugsrud's death referred to him as the "father of pro football in Minnesota." At the time of his death, he still owned 10 percent of the Vikings.

Haugsrud, who owned a candy and tobacco wholesale distributorship in Duluth for many years, was the senior committee nominee for the Pro Football Hall of Fame in 1973 but was not elected. He is a member of the Wisconsin-Superior (his alma mater) Athletic Hall of Fame.

13

BOBBY BELL

A TWO-SPORT PIONEER AT
THE UNIVERSITY OF MINNESOTA

The first African American to play football for the University of Minnesota was Bobby Marshall, who lettered for the Gophers from 1904 to 1906. Marshall, who was born in Milwaukee, Wisconsin, and raised in Minneapolis, was the first Black football player in the Western (later called the Big Ten) Conference. In 1905, Marshall became the first Black athlete to be named an All-American in football. In 1920, he became the first African American to play in the National Football League.

After Marshall graduated, it was twenty years before the next Black athlete played football for the Gophers. During the 1930s, several African Americans played for the Gophers, but it wasn't until the late 1950s that the first Black players received athletic scholarships to play football for the Gophers.

Bobby Bell, who had played six-man football for a small, segregated high school in Shelby, North Carolina, was one of the first Black players—along with Judge Dickson, Bob McNeil, Bill Munsey and Sandy Stephens—to be recruited by Gophers football coach Murray Warmath.

Because major college football programs in the South in the 1950s weren't recruiting Black players, a North Carolina coach recommended Bell to Warmath.

During his Gophers football career, Bell helped the team win a national championship as they made back-to-back appearances in the Rose Bowl. Through the 2021 season, the appearances in 1961 and 1962 Rose Bowls are the only times the school has played in the prestigious New Year's Day

Bobby Bell, a member of the College Football and Pro Football Halls of Fame, also played basketball for the University of Minnesota. *University of Minnesota.*

bowl game in Pasadena, California. Following his senior season in 1962, Bell was awarded the Outland Trophy, given annually to the top interior lineman in college football.

Warmath described Bell as "the greatest lineman I have ever seen."

Following his Gophers career, Bell was drafted by the Minnesota Vikings of the NFL and the Kansas City Chiefs of the rival AFL. Bell signed with the Chiefs and went on to play twelve professional seasons.

Among his accomplishments with the Gopher football program, one detail is often overlooked about Bell's athletic career at Minnesota. He was the first African American to play basketball for the university. In addition to playing football at Cleveland High School, which had an enrollment of 168 students, the six-foot, four-inch Bell was a standout basketball player. As a senior, he averaged 26 points per game.

During his first year at the University of Minnesota—freshmen were ineligible to play varsity sports at that time—Bell was a quarterback for the freshman football team and played on an intramural basketball team.

Bell enjoyed several highlights during his first year on the Minneapolis campus. According to a report in the November 21, 1959 edition of the *Minneapolis Star*, Bell, "who reportedly can throw a football close to 90 yards played up to his 6-4 size and was the big star of the Minnesota freshmen's intra-squad game in the field house Friday afternoon." Bell threw a touchdown pass in the game, which ended in a 6–6 tie.

Three months later, in the March 11, 1960 edition of the *Minneapolis Tribune*, columnist Sid Hartman wrote, "Bobby Bell, Gopher gridder, scored 40 points Wednesday night as Territorial Hall defeated the Phi Epsilon Kappa team for the All-University basketball crown. The 6-4 Bell may be a candidate for John Kundla's Gopher five next year."

In the fall of 1960, Bell was part of a big turnaround for the Gopher football program. The team had won just 3 of 18 games over the previous two years, and many fans were calling for Warmath to be fired.

The Gophers won their first 7 games in 1960. The 7th game was a 27–10 victory over No. 1 Iowa in Minneapolis. The next week, the Gophers suffered a 23–14 loss to Purdue, which was quarterbacked by future

Minnesota Twins infielder Bernie Allen. It was the Gophers' only regular-season loss. The team finished the regular season with a 26–7 victory over Wisconsin. Their season ended with a 17–7 loss to Washington in the Rose Bowl on January 2, 1961.

One week after the Rose Bowl, the Associated Press reported, "Bobby Bell reports to Johnny Kundla's distressed basketball team today." The *Minneapolis Star* wrote, "Bobby Bell is due to join the cagers. And that might help."

Bell joined the Gophers basketball team in its second season under Kundla, who had coached the Minneapolis Lakers to five league titles. At the time, the team had a 2-8 record. Two days before Bell joined, the Gophers lost at Iowa, 71–46.

Bell did not play in the Gophers' 65–64 loss to Purdue on January 14 in Minneapolis. Two nights later, he played two minutes in the team's 66–54 victory over Northwestern at Williams Arena. Bell missed his only field-goal attempt and didn't score.

According to Dick Gordon in the *Minneapolis Star*: "The crowd of 6,018 obviously liked Bobby Bell, who was greeted by tremendous applause when he made his official switch from football to basketball late in the game. A charging foul robbed Robert of a basket but by then, of course, that made no difference."

Bell didn't play in the Gophers' next game, on January 21 at Ohio State. The Buckeyes, the top-ranked team in the country, defeated the Gophers, 75–56. Ohio, whose roster included future NBA stars John Havlicek and Jerry Lucas and future coaching legend Bob Knight, improved to 12-0 with the victory. The Buckeyes were 26-0 when they lost to Cincinnati in the NCAA championship game.

On January 23, Bell scored 4 points in Minnesota's 89–70 victory over Michigan State at Williams Arena. Gordon wrote in the *Minneapolis Star* that Bell "once again was the favorite of the crowd of 5,506." Bell told Gordon, "I'm still a little shaky and didn't think my first free throw attempt would make the rim."

Bell appeared in only one of the Gophers' final 9 games. On February 11, he didn't score in the team's 70–53 victory over Michigan at Williams Arena.

Minneapolis newspapers did not mention the significance of Bell's two months with the team.

Later in 1961, Archie Clark, Lou Hudson and Don Yates became the first African Americans to be offered scholarships to play basketball for the Gophers. They joined the team as sophomores in the 1962–63 season. Clark, like Bell, was a multisport standout. He was the starting center fielder on the Gophers' 1964 baseball team, which won the College World Series. Clark and Hudson went on to have lengthy careers in the NBA.

In 1965, LeRoy Gardner, a six-foot, four-inch forward on the St. Paul Central team that won the third-place game at the state tournament, became the first Black player born and raised in Minnesota to receive a full athletic scholarship to play basketball for the Gophers.

After his two-month stint with the university's basketball team, Bell concentrated on football for the rest of his college athletic career.

He earned numerous honors for his college and professional football careers. He was named to the NFL's All-Decade team for the 1970s. He was elected to the Pro Football Hall of Fame in 1983 and to the College Football Hall of Fame in 1991.

In 1999, the *Minneapolis Star Tribune* named an "all-time" team for Gophers football. Bell was one of eleven players named to the team.

The *Star Tribune* said of Bell, "Undersized even before the era of line-playing behemoths, Bell's quickness, upper body strength and flat out speed caused Butch Nash [an assistant Gophers coach from 1947 to 1991] to make this sincere and overwhelming statement: 'He was the best football player we've ever had here.'"

In 2013, Bell was honored in a ceremony in Shelby, North Carolina, as a "Hometown Hall of Famer." He summed up his career for the *Charlotte Observer*: "It's incredible that a kid who played six-man football could have the career I was able to have."

When Bell left the university in 1963 to sign with the Kansas City Chiefs, he was thirteen credits short of completing his college degree. When he left North Carolina, he promised his family that he would earn a college degree. He eventually did.

In December 2014, Bell finished the coursework for the thirteen credits and earned his college degree at the age of seventy-four.

14

INFINITY

A STATISTICAL ODDITY

One of baseball's statistical rarities is an Earned Run Average (ERA) of "infinity." An ERA of infinity happens when a pitcher records no outs while allowing earned runs.

Of the more than twenty thousand players who have appeared in a Major League Baseball game, nineteen pitchers have been documented with a career ERA of infinity. Three of those pitchers—Fred Bruckbauer and Elmer "Doc" Hamann, who were born in New Ulm, and Gordin Sundin, born in Minneapolis—are Minnesota natives. Bruckbauer and Sundin are two of the three most recent players to "achieve" the oddity.

Before their shared statistical anomaly, each of these players was a highly sought pitching prospect.

Hamann, who was born in December 1900, was a standout in basketball and baseball in New Ulm. As a high school senior in 1921, the six-foot, one-inch Hamann helped New Ulm reach the championship game of the boys' state basketball tournament, held at Carleton College in Northfield, Minnesota.

In the championship game on March 18, Minneapolis Central edged New Ulm, 19–15, for the title. Hamann scored 13 of New Ulm's 15 points and was named to the All-Tournament team.

During the summer of 1921, Hamann pitched for a semipro team in New Ulm. In September 1921, he enrolled at St. Thomas College (now the University of St. Thomas) with the intention of majoring in accounting.

In his first year at St. Thomas, Hamann played basketball and baseball. Among his highlights for the baseball team, in the spring of 1922, Hamann pitched a two-hit shutout as St. Thomas defeated the University of Minnesota on Northrop Field on April 20. The *Minneapolis Tribune* wrote, "Big Doc Hamann of St. Thomas college had too much on the ball." Hamann struck out 8 in the 1–0 victory and went 1-for-3 at the plate. St. Thomas went on to win the state college conference title.

Hamann spent the summer pitching in his hometown before being offered a tryout at the end of the summer by the Cleveland Indians of the American League. The *Minneapolis Tribune* reported on September 13, 1922, that Hamann, "one of the best state college twirlers in the conference will get a tryout with the Cleveland American League baseball team it was announced yesterday. Hamann left yesterday to join the Indians immediately."

The *New Ulm Review* wrote in its September 13 edition: "Hamann is a wonderful pitcher. At times he may be slightly wild, but he makes up for that in speed and break. Hamann has been the biggest star in an all-star team this season and his going will be felt by the local team."

Eight days later, Hamann made his only major-league appearance. On September 21, in a day game at Cleveland's Dunn Field, the Indians, who had a 4-game winning streak, were trailing the Boston Red Sox, 9–5, going into the ninth inning. Cleveland manager (and future National Baseball Hall of Fame member) Tris Speaker sent Hamann into the game. Hamann, the fourth Cleveland pitcher, faced seven hitters without getting any outs. He allowed 3 hits, walked 3 and hit 1 batter. He also threw a wild pitch before being removed by Speaker. Six of the hitters eventually scored as the Red Sox won, 15–5.

In the box score of the game published in newspapers the next day, Hamann's name was misspelled "Haman."

In November 1922, the *New Ulm Review* wrote that the Indians had offered Hamann a contract and invited him to spring training in 1923, but he declined the offer and returned to school at St. Thomas. He rejoined the baseball team for the 1923 season.

Eligibility rules were clearly different then. Even if someone had played professional baseball, it was possible to play for a college team that wasn't part of a major conference like the Big Ten. Eligibility standards were set by the conferences, not by a national administrative organization.

For example, Dick Siebert, who coached baseball at the University of Minnesota from 1948 to 1978, made his professional baseball debut in 1929 following his first season at Concordia Junior College (now

Concordia University) in St. Paul. He returned to Concordia after the season and played for Concordia again in 1930.

Hamann's return to the St. Thomas baseball team was cut short. In its May 24, 1923 edition, the *Minneapolis Tribune* reported that the "crack St. Thomas battery" of Hamann and "Jiggs" Donaghue "have played their last game with the Cadet baseball team." The players were ruled ineligible after the school learned that they had played in an "independent baseball game at Austin, Minn." the previous weekend. Hamann and Donaghue were "immediately requested to turn in their uniforms."

The school said the appearance by Hamann and Donaghue in the game "had violated the eligibilty rules of the conference." According to the report, the two players "composed the strongest battery in the conference, the former working well in all his games so far this season."

Two months later, Hamann was in the news again. The *Minneapolis Tribune* reported on July 22 that Hamann had signed a contract with the Minneapolis Millers. Since leaving St. Thomas, he had been pitching for Watertown (South Dakota) in the four-team Class D Dakota League.

The newspaper wrote that Hamann, "the former St. Thomas twirler and later with a Dakota League club, is expected to get into a Minneapolis uniform today."

The next day, the *Minneapolis Star* wrote that he would be given a tryout by the Millers on their upcoming road trip. (The paper misspelled his name "Hamman.")

On August 1, in the second game of a doubleheader in Toledo, Ohio, Hamann made his debut for the Millers. The *Minneapolis Star* reported: "After winning the fifth straight game from Toledo by bagging the first of two yesterday by a score of 6 to 4, Joe Cantillon gave his kid pitchers, Clarence Griffin and Doc Hamman [*sic*] a chance. The young hurlers didn't do so well, being bounced for a 14–3 defeat."

Hamann, the third of three Millers pitchers, allowed 9 hits and 3 runs in three innings.

The next mention of Hamann by a Minneapolis newspaper is on August 11, when the *Minneapolis Tribune* said, "Doc Hamman [*sic*] has a lot of stuff but he can't handle it." That was last mention of Hamann for the rest of the 1923 season. He is not listed in the season-ending statistics for the Millers, who had a 74-92 record in 1923. But in that era, players who appeared in fewer than 10 games were often not included.

Sundin earned All-State honors in baseball, basketball and football at Minneapolis Washburn High School in the 1950s. In his senior year at

Washburn, he was named the top player in the Minneapolis City Conference after scoring 14 touchdowns for the Washburn football team. In basketball, the six-foot, four-inch Sundin helped the Millers win the state title, and in baseball, his pitching helped the Millers win the state title in that sport as well. Washburn was the first school in Minnesota history to win state basketball and baseball titles in the same school year.

During his baseball career at Washburn, he went 20-1 and threw 5 no-hitters. *Minneapolis Tribune* columnist Sid Hartman wrote of Sundin: "He could do it all. Gordie was one of the best all-around athletes to ever come out of Minneapolis. He could have played college football. He was recruited by the Gophers, Notre Dame and Wisconsin."

Two months after his high school graduation, he agreed to a contract with the Baltimore Orioles, which included a signing bonus of $50,000. Sundin reported to the team's York, Pennsylvania farm team in the Class B Piedmont League. For the remainder of the season, he appeared in 5 games, going 1-2 for the White Roses, whose roster included future Hall of Famer Brooks Robinson.

When Sundin joined the Orioles in Scottsdale, Arizona, in February 1956 for spring training, he was the youngest player on their roster at eighteen. But Sundin, who had been dealing with a sore elbow, was sidelined early on during spring training because of the issue and underwent surgery in early March.

He spent the next six months going through rehabilitation. In its September 2, 1956 issue, the *Baltimore Sun* reported that Sundin had rejoined the team: "Even though [Orioles general manager Paul] Richards says now that he does not intend to work Sundin in a regular game, it wouldn't be too surprising to see the huge right-hander get a trial before the season ends."

The report went on to say, "He has also been working on his breaking pitches without any pain in his elbow and it is no secret that everybody concerned with the Orioles has high hopes for Sundin."

While Sundin was recovering from the surgery, Richards told *The Sporting News* that surgery had fixed Sundin's elbow problem and added: "He can throw right through a brick wall when he really lets go. When he develops control, he will be a great one."

On September 19, 1956, a cool, damp day in Detroit, Sundin entered the game in the eighth inning with the Orioles trailing the Tigers, 8–1. After walking the first hitters he faced—Tigers pitcher Frank Lary and Harvey Kuenn, who led the AL in hits in 1956—Sundin fell behind in the count, 2-and-1, to Jack Phillips. At that point, Orioles manager Lum Harris sent

Billy O'Dell in to relieve Sundin. Sundin had thrown just 1 strike in the 11 pitches he delivered. Lary eventually scored on a sacrifice fly by Al Kaline as the Tigers won the game, 9–1.

It was Sundin's last major-league appearance. He continued to pitch professionally for the next five seasons, reaching Triple-A (the highest classification in minor-league baseball) three times before retiring at the age of twenty-three.

When he was healthy, Sundin was considered one of the hardest throwers in professional baseball. He told the *Baltimore Sun* in 2006: "It was between me and Herb Score [of the Cleveland Indians] on who threw the hardest. They didn't have all the [radar] guns they have now, but Score was approaching 100 mph and I was approaching Score, so you can take it from there."

Asked in the interview about his career ERA, Sundin replied, "There's nothing I can do about it. I might as well grin and bear it."

Shortly after the 1956 season, Sundin married Mary Ann Dorsey, an alumna of Washburn High School. At the 1956 Winter Olympics in Cortina d'Ampezzo, Italy, Dorsey was an alternate on the U.S. figure skating team.

In 1961, while Sundin was in his final professional season, Bruckbauer made one appearance for the Minnesota Twins.

Bruckbauer, who was born in New Ulm but grew up in nearby Sleepy Eye, Minnesota, went 16-5 in two seasons for the Minnesota Gophers before signing with the Washington Senators in 1959. After receiving a reported $30,000 signing bonus from the Senators, Bruckbauer reported to Fox Cities of the Three-I League. He had a solid inaugural season in professional baseball, going 12-5 with a 2.89 ERA in 20 games. He completed 10 of his 18 starts and threw 4 shutouts.

Bruckbauer went to spring training with the Senators in 1960 but started to experience pain in his right shoulder. But after being sent to Charlotte of the Class A South Atlantic League, his season started out on a positive note. In his first start of the season, he took a no-hitter into the eighth inning in an eventual 6–3 victory over Columbia in Charlotte. But the issue with his shoulder limited him to just 76 innings in 1960 as he went 4-5 in 17 appearances (12 starts).

In 1961, Bruckbauer made the Minnesota Twins' Opening Day roster. In its April 16 edition, the *Minneapolis Tribune* produced a special section for the team's first season in Minnesota with brief bios of each player on the roster. The *Tribune* wrote of Bruckbauer, "Troubled by a sore arm, he had his tonsils removed last winter in the hope of ending his arm trouble."

The Twins opened their season on April 11 with a 6–0 victory over the defending American League champion New York Yankees in New York. The Twins won 8 of their first 10 games, but Bruckbauer didn't appear in a game in that season-opening stretch.

In their 11th game, on April 25 in Kansas City, the Athletics pounded seven Twins pitchers for 16 hits in a 20–2 victory. Bruckbauer made his major-league debut in the fourth inning. He faced four hitters, allowing 3 hits, 2 runs and 1 walk. After Lou Klimchock doubled, Bruckbauer was replaced by Chuck Stobbs.

Bruckbauer was sent back to the minors for the rest of the 1961 season, where he went 7-10 in 30 games with Syracuse of the Triple-A International League.

He started the 1962 season with Charlotte but was released in early May after pitching just 19 innings. "I had a gut feeling my arm wasn't coming around," Bruckbauer told the *Minneapolis Star Tribune* in 2007, "and it never did."

Hamann died in January 1973 at the age of seventy-two, Bruckbauer died in October 2007 at sixty-nine and Sundin died in May 2016 at seventy-eight.

15

TOMMY WILLIAMS

A HOCKEY PIONEER

During the 2021–22 National Hockey League season, 61 players born in Minnesota appeared in an NHL game. At the conclusion of the season, 297 Minnesota natives—more than any other state—had played in the NHL in the league's history.

But prior to the NHL's expansion from six to twelve teams in 1967, Minnesotans—or any American-born player—were a rarity in the league.

Prior to 1967, there were only one hundred players on the rosters of the league's original six teams: Boston, Chicago, Detroit, Montreal, New York Rangers and Toronto. Before the 1965–66 season, NHL teams could dress just sixteen skaters and one goaltender for league games. Beginning with the 1965–66 season, NHL teams were required to dress sixteen skaters and two goaltenders. The game-day roster was subsequently expanded to seventeen skaters in 1971 and eighteen in 1982.

Even with the limited roster spots, it is still surprising that for much of the 1960s, there was only one American-born player in the NHL: Duluth, Minnesota native Tommy Williams.

Williams played high school hockey for Duluth Central High School before being selected to play for the 1960 United States Olympic team. The nineteen-year-old played a significant role for the U.S. team, which won the gold medal—the first for a U.S. Olympic hockey team—at the games played in Squaw Valley, California.

Williams assisted on the game-winning goal, scored by Minnesotan Billy Christian, in the 3–2 victory over Russia in the gold medal game.

John Mariucci was an All-American in hockey for the University of Minnesota before playing in the NHL for five seasons. *University of Minnesota*.

After the Olympics, Williams, who had originally intended to play college hockey for the University of Minnesota, signed with the Boston Bruins of the NHL. After one season with Kingston, the Bruins' minor-league affiliate in the Eastern League, Williams made his NHL debut on October 11, 1961, in Boston's 1961–62 season opener.

Williams was returned to Kingston after the game. But after 36 games with Kingston, he joined the Bruins for good in January 1962. After a brief appearance against Toronto on January 21, he scored his first 2 NHL goals in the Bruins' 5–3 victory over the Chicago Blackhawks on January 27 in Boston.

Williams became the first American-born player to compete for the Bruins since Minnesota native Frank Brimsek in 1949 and the first American-born player to play regularly in the NHL since Brimsek retired in 1950.

Former University of Minnesota goaltender Jack McCartan, a teammate of Williams on the 1960 U.S. Olympic team, appeared in 4 games with the New York Rangers right after the Olympics in March 1960 and then in 8 games during the 1960–61 season.

The first native Minnesotan to play in the NHL was Elwyn "Doc" Romnes. Romnes, who was born in White Bear Lake, began his career with the Chicago Blackhawks in 1927. He was one of two American-born players in the NHL that season. Romnes went on to play eleven seasons in the NHL. For a brief period in the early 1930s, there were fifteen American-born players in the league. Romnes helped the Blackhawks win the Stanley Cup in 1934 to become the first Minnesotan to be on a Stanley Cup–winning team.

When Brimsek joined the Boston Bruins in 1938, he became just the second American in the NHL that season. The other was Minnesota-native Mike Karakas of the Blackhawks. Both Brimsek and Karakas were born in Eveleth. When Karakas debuted with the Blackhawks in 1935, the other American-born player in the league was Donnie McFayden.

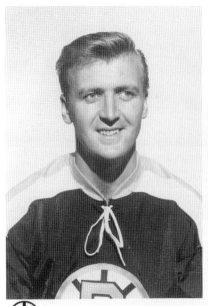

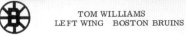
TOM WILLIAMS
LEFT WING   BOSTON BRUINS

1938-1939 BOSTON BRUINS — No. 1 — **FRANK BRIMSEK**, GOAL — AGE 21, WGT. 180, HGT. 5:11 — HOME, EVELETH, MINNESOTA

Opposite, top: For the first half of the 1960s, Tommy Williams was the only American-born player in the NHL. *Boston Bruins*.

Opposite, bottom: Frank Brimsek, who made his NHL debut in 1938, was named to the NHL All-Star team eight times. *U.S. Hockey Hall of Fame*.

Above: Mike Karakas made his NHL debut with the Chicago Blackhawks in 1935. *U.S. Hockey Hall of Fame*.

Within two years of Brimsek joining the Bruins, two more Eveleth natives made it to the NHL: Sam LoPresti and John Mariucci. LoPresti set an NHL record on March 4, 1941, when he had 80 saves against the Bruins in the Blackhawks' 3–2 loss to Boston. In the 1970s, LoPresti's son Pete played for the Minnesota North Stars for five seasons.

Williams finished the 1961–62 season with the Bruins, scoring 6 goals in 27 games. He played for the Bruins until 1969. In May 1969, he was traded to the North Stars, one of the six franchises added by the league before the 1967–68 season.

Midway through his second season with the North Stars, Williams was traded to the California Golden Seals. He finished the 1970–71 season with California and, after spending the 1971–72 season with the Golden Seals, signed to play with New England of the World Hockey Association (WHA). After two seasons with New England, he returned to the NHL and spent the last two seasons of his sixteen-year professional career with the Washington Capitals.

At the time of his retirement in 1976, his NHL totals of 169 goals and 430 total points put him at the top of those two career categories among American-born players in NHL history. He also scored 31 goals in 139 games in his two seasons in the WHA.

Among Minnesota-born players, through the 2021–22 season, Zach Parise is the all-time leader in goals scored (408), and Phil Housley is the leader in games played (1,495), assists (894) and points (1,232).

In October 1981, Williams was inducted into the U.S. Hockey Hall of Fame, which is located in Eveleth.

In his biography on the Hall of Fame's website, Williams said, "I played before expansion. I played because I was good at it and I was fortunate to do something for a long number of years that I enjoyed. How many guys can say they enjoyed a job for 16 years?"

Williams died on February 8, 1992, at the age of fifty-one.

16

TERRY DILLON

A PROMISING FOOTBALL CAREER CUT SHORT

Terry Dillon spent just one season with the Minnesota Vikings. During his brief career with the team—7 games in 1963—Dillon left an indelible impression on the organization.

Dillon, who was born on August 18, 1941, in Waukesha, Wisconsin, started playing football in junior high in Fargo, North Dakota. He attended high school in the Minneapolis suburb of Hopkins.

At Hopkins, he earned eight athletic letters and was named All-Lake Conference in football twice. After graduating from Hopkins High School in 1959, he enrolled at the University of Montana in Missoula. With the Grizzlies, he was a two-way starter, at running back and defensive back, for three seasons (1960–62).

As a senior, the five-foot, nine-inch, 194-pounder led the Grizzlies in rushing and tackles. He rushed for 892 yards in 10 games—the fifth-best total in program history up to that point—and averaged 5.2 yards per carry. That figure was fourth-best in the nation.

After his senior season, he played in the East-West Shrine Game, an All-Star game for the top seniors in the nation played annually at Kezar Stadium in San Francisco

Prior to playing in the bowl game, Dillon was selected by the Oakland Raiders in the eighteenth round of the AFL draft. He was one of the standouts for the West team in the All-Star game, intercepting a pass thrown by future NFL quarterback Daryle Lamonica and returning it 20 yards in the fourth quarter.

After the game, Dillon, who had not been selected in the NFL draft, got offers from the Raiders of the AFL and the Vikings and the San Francisco 49ers of the NFL before signing a free-agent contract with the Vikings.

Norm Kragseth, Dillon's football coach at Hopkins High School, brought him to the Vikings' attention. Kragseth was working in the Vikings' scouting department, and his main duty was watching film of players from small colleges.

In July 1963, Dillon was among fifty rookies and first-year players who joined Vikings' veterans and reported for training camp in Bemidji, Minnesota. Dillon stood out right away. The headline above the *Minneapolis Tribune*'s story about the first day of camp read, "Dillon Impresses in Vikings Drills."

Reporter Jim Klobuchar wrote that the day's activities "produced a surprising performance by Hopkins's Terry Dillon. Dillon may make a serious run for a job in the secondary....Dillon displayed quickness in the pass defense drills and then sped the 50-yard time trial distance in a totally unexpected 5.7 seconds in full gear, matching second-year speedster Bobby Reed as the fastest in camp."

Klobuchar went on to write, "For an added flourish of versatility, Dillon punted pretty well."

Vikings coach Norm Van Brocklin told reporters, "We are a long way from judgement, but for pure physical appearance and action, Dillon reminds you a lot of Yale Lary of Detroit."

In 1963, Lary, a defensive back, was beginning the next-to-last season of his eleven-year NFL career, which saw him named to the NFL's All-Decade team for the 1950s and eventually earn him a spot in the Pro Football Hall of Fame.

Dillon, who didn't play in the Vikings' first two preseason games, made his debut for the team in its 17–16 victory over the New York Giants in a preseason game at Metropolitan Stadium on August 25. Six days later, he suffered a severe ankle sprain in the Vikings' 34–27 loss to the Philadelphia Eagles in a preseason game in Hershey, Pennsylvania. That injury cost Dillon a spot on the Vikings' forty-player Opening Day roster.

Van Brocklin told reporters, "We admire Dillon, but we just got into a roster bind."

About halfway through training camp, the Vikings had picked up a rookie defensive back named Karl Kassulke after he had been cut by the Detroit Lions. Kassulke went on to play for the Vikings for ten seasons before being paralyzed from injuries suffered in a motorcycle accident in July 1973. The accident occurred when Kassulke, who was thirty-two at the time, was on his way to training camp in Mankato, Minnesota.

After cutting Dillon, the Vikings re-signed him to their taxi (practice) squad. Dillon spent the first half of the 1963 season on the taxi squad.

On October 31, the Vikings placed flanker Ray Poage on injured reserve after he suffered a thigh injury and activated Dillon to fill the spot. The Vikings also announced that Dillon would be in their starting lineup three days later against the Los Angeles Rams.

Dillon, who became the first graduate of a Twin Cities high school to make the Vikings roster for a regular-season game, told reporters, "It's quite a shock, and what a thrill."

Vikings defensive assistant coach Harry Gilmer told reporters: "The thing I like about the boy has been his willingness to learn. Even after being cut, he has shown this."

The Vikings defeated the Rams, 21–13, to end a 4-game losing streak. After the game, Gilmer told Sid Hartman of the *Minneapolis Tribune* that Dillon hadn't made any serious errors in the game.

Dillon told Hartman, "I've learned a lot of football since I reported at Bemidji [in July]. We had always played a zone defense in college. This man-to-man defense wasn't easy for me. I was a little nervous at the start. But once the game started, I was okay. This was an opportunity that I didn't know I'd ever get. Now that I got the chance to play, I didn't want to hurt myself."

Dillon remained in the starting lineup for the Vikings' final 7 games. The Vikings, who were 5-8-1 in 1963 (their third season in the NFL), were 3-3-1 in the 7 games Dillon started.

After his rookie season, Dillon signed a contract with the Vikings for 1964 and returned to Missoula, Montana, to work a construction job.

On May 28, 1964, he was part of a crew working on a bridge construction project twenty-five miles west of Missoula. Dillon fell into the Clark Fork River when part of a temporary deck on the bridge gave way. Witnesses said Dillon, who survived the fifty-foot drop to the river, battled the strong current of the river before disappearing in the current.

His body wasn't found for almost two months. On July 17, a fisherman found his body about seventeen miles downstream from the bridge. Dillon was twenty-two at the time of the accident.

Van Brocklin told the *Minneapolis Tribune*: "I really don't want to talk about the Vikings' loss. It is a terrible loss for his parents and family, and for anybody who knew Terry Dillon well. Such a wonderful kid. He had the perfect temperament to play safety in the NFL. He wanted to learn, and he learned quickly."

Van Brocklin said that during his 7-game stint in 1963, Dillon played "as well as any rookie in a tough league could ever hope to play the position."

Gilmer said that Dillon "was going to be one of the fine defensive players in the league."

Dillon's alma mater retired his jersey number (22) and initiated an award named after Dillon. Montana presents the award annually to an outstanding defensive back or receiver.

Following the 1964 season, the Vikings started a team award named after Dillon. The award was for the player who displayed ability, dedication and self-sacrifice. The first recipient was linebacker Rip Hawkins.

Van Brocklin told the *Minneapolis Tribune*: "The Viking coaching staff joins in saluting Rip Hawkins on the occasion of this award. We cannot think of a man more deserving. Terry Dillon represented the best in devotion to the squad. He was a player of ability and character. He would have become one of the stars in the National Football League. Rip Hawkins gave us those qualities."

The Vikings retired the award in the early 2000s.

17

THE ABA'S CHAOTIC TWO YEARS
IN THE TWIN CITIES

George Mikan, a member of the Naismith Basketball Hall of Fame and one of the top fifty players in National Basketball Association (NBA) history, helped the Minneapolis Lakers become the league's first dynasty.

After the Lakers franchise was moved to Los Angeles following the 1959–60 season, the Twin Cities was without an NBA team for nearly three decades. Mikan played a big role in bringing the NBA back.

In 1984, Minnesota governor Rudy Perpich formed a task force to see if an NBA team could succeed in the Twin Cities. Mikan was named to lead the task force, and the efforts paid off two years later, when the NBA awarded an expansion franchise to Minnesota. The Minnesota Timberwolves began play in 1989.

During the twenty-nine years Minnesota was without an NBA team, the Twin Cities did have a brief, two-year experience with professional basketball. Mikan played a big role in that as well.

On February 2, 1967, the formation of a second professional basketball league was announced in New York. The league, named the American Basketball Association (ABA), would begin play in the fall of 1967. One of the league's eleven franchises was to be located in the Twin Cities. The other franchises were awarded to Anaheim, Dallas, Denver, Indiana, Houston, Kentucky, New Jersey, New Orleans, Oakland and Pittsburgh.

At the news conference, the league also introduced Mikan as its commissioner. Mikan, a lawyer by trade who was running a travel agency in the Twin Cities, announced that the league office would be in the Twin Cities.

The state's franchise, which was named the Minnesota Muskies, made big news before it played its first game. On April 2, with its first pick in the league's inaugural draft, the team selected University of New Mexico center Mel Daniels. A month later, Daniels was selected in the first round of the NBA draft by the Cincinnati Royals. In early June, Daniels signed with the Muskies.

The Muskies selected University of North Dakota forward Phil Jackson in the second round of the draft and got into a bidding war for Jackson with the NBA's New York Knicks, who had taken Jackson in the second round. He signed with the Knicks and went on to play twelve years in the NBA before embarking on a coaching career.

Connie Hawkins averaged 30.2 points per game for the Minnesota Pipers during the 1968–69 ABA season. *Minnesota Pipers.*

On May 17, the Muskies announced that they had signed former Gopher Lou Hudson to a three-year contract. Hudson had just finished his rookie season of professional basketball, averaging 17.9 points per game for the St. Louis Hawks of the NBA. The Hawks, who said Hudson was still under contract to them, sued the Muskies. Hudson returned to the Hawks for the 1967–68 season. Following that campaign, the Hawks moved to Atlanta.

The Muskies played their first game on October 22, 1967, losing to the Kentucky Colonels before 8,104 at Metropolitan Sports Center in Bloomington. The night before, the expansion Minnesota North Stars played their first NHL home game, defeating the California Seals, 3–1, before 12,951.

The Muskies, led by Daniels, who averaged 22.2 points and 15.6 rebounds per game and earned ABA Rookie of the Year honors, went 50-28 during the regular season to finish in second place in the ABA's Eastern Division.

In the playoffs, the Muskies defeated Kentucky, 3-2, in the first round before losing to the Pittsburgh Pipers, 4-1, in the Eastern Division finals. The Pipers went on to defeat the New Orleans Buccaneers, 4-3, to win the first ABA title.

Following the inaugural season, both the Muskies and Pipers moved. In May, the Muskies announced they were moving to Miami, where they would become the Miami Floridians. Muskies ownership cited low attendance (about 2,500 per game) and overall losses of a reported $400,000 as reasons for the move.

But the Twin Cities was without an ABA team for just one month. In late June, William J. Erickson, a Twin Cities businessman and attorney, purchased a majority interest in the champion Pipers and announced he would move the team to Minnesota for the 1968–69 season. The Pipers had lost a reported $250,000 in their first season.

The relocation of the Pipers to Minnesota presented Upper Midwest basketball fans the opportunity to watch Connie Hawkins, one of the league's best players and a future Hall of Famer.

The circumstances that brought Hawkins to the ABA were controversial. Hawkins, from Brooklyn, New York, enrolled at the University of Iowa in the fall of 1960. During his freshman season, news of a point-shaving / gambling scandal in college basketball was reported in New York City.

Hawkins's name was mentioned in the investigation because he was known to several of those suspected in the scandal. Even though he was not implicated or charged, Hawkins was expelled from Iowa.

No other college program offered a scholarship, and the NBA said it would not approve any contract for him when he became eligible for the draft in 1964. In 1966, the league officially banned Hawkins. As a result, he played one season with the Pittsburgh Rens in the ABL and three seasons with the Harlem Globetrotters before signing with the Pittsburgh Pipers in 1967. While playing for the Globetrotters, he sued the NBA, saying the league had banned him unfairly because there was no credible evidence he had been involved in any gambling activities.

The Minnesota Pipers opened their season at home on October 27, 1968, against Metropolitan Sports Center's previous basketball tenant. The Pipers defeated the former Minnesota Muskies—now the Miami Floridians—126–94. The sparse crowd of 1,943 witnessed Chico Vaughan and Willie Porter each score 23 points and Hawkins contribute 21.

The season got off to a good start for the Pipers but soon turned chaotic. The team had scheduled to play 10 of its regular-season home games in Duluth, 150 miles north of the Twin Cities, in an effort to build regional interest.

On Tuesday, November 19, in their 3rd game in Duluth, the Pipers lost to Denver, 126–121, at the Duluth Arena before 652 fans. Hawkins was the positive note for the Muskies, scoring 39 points. In their first 2 games in Duluth, the Pipers had drawn crowds of 1,665 and 1,299.

After the game, Pipers president Bill Erickson told reporters he was reconsidering his plan to have the team play 10 games in Duluth. "We don't have to play 10 dates here," he said. "But remember, we want to give the Duluth fans a fair trial. It's still November. What is a fair trial?"

In the two weeks after the loss to Denver in Duluth, the twenty-six-year-old Hawkins provided two of the season's highlights. On November 27, he scored an ABA single-game record 57 points in the Pipers' 110–101 victory over the New York Nets in New York. Hawkins, whose previous high-scoring total in an ABA game was 45 (in the league's first season), broke the ABA record of 54 set by Louie Dampier of the Kentucky Colonels the previous March.

Hawkins, who scored 28 points in the first half, made 19 of 27 field-goal attempts and 19 of 25 free throws. The six-foot, eight-inch Hawkins also led the Pipers with 17 rebounds. The victory was the Pipers' 9th in their 13 games to that point.

On December 5 in a 119–118 loss to the Nuggets in Denver, Hawkins scored 53 points, setting an ABA record for field goals made (20). He became the first player in the league to score at least 50 points twice. Even though the loss ended the Muskies' 7-game winning streak, they still led the Eastern Division with a 14-5 record.

Hawkins, who had won the scoring title in the ABA's first season with an average of 26.8 points per game, was averaging 34.3 points after the game in Denver.

In late December, the *Minneapolis Tribune* wrote about the Pipers' attendance issues. In 16 home games—10 at the Metropolitan Sports Center and 6 in Duluth—the team drew 37,175 fans, an average of 2,322 per game. In the games at the Metropolitan Sports Center, the team drew 27,080 fans. In the contests in Duluth, the team drew just 10,077—1,680 per game.

On January 22, the team announced that it was canceling its last 2 scheduled games in Duluth. In 8 games in the Port City, the team averaged 1,500 fans per game.

On the court, the team was dealing with injuries. Hawkins, who scored at least 30 points in 16 consecutive games in one stretch, suffered a knee injury in practice on January 15. The Pipers had an Eastern Division–leading record of 24-15 at the time. Three other starters for the Pipers—Art Heyman, Vaughn and Tom Washington—missed games because of injuries.

The same week as Hawkins's injury, reports surfaced in Twin Cities newspapers that the Pipers would move after the season. A headline in the January 14, 1969 edition of the *Minneapolis Star* read, "Speculation Increases: Pipers Moving to Jersey City Site?" The accompanying story reported, "Latest word—denied by the team and the league—is that the

Minnesota franchise will transfer to Jersey City after this season." Erickson told the newspaper there was "no substance to the report" and that the Pipers would finish the season in Minnesota and be in the state for the 1969–70 season.

The low point of the season for the franchise occurred on January 28 in Louisville, Kentucky. Pipers coach Jim Harding, who was in Louisville to coach the Eastern Division in the ABA's All-Star Game, and Gabe Rubin, one of the Pipers' owners, got into a fight in their hotel's lobby. Two days later, Harding was fired as coach and replaced by Gus Young.

In early March, in an attempt to draw more fans, the team announced that it was lowering the price of all tickets to two dollars.

Hawkins, who underwent surgery on his knee on February 1, returned to the Pipers' lineup in early March. The team played its final regular-season home game on March 25 at the St. Paul Auditorium. The Pipers defeated New York, 114–104, in front of 1,130. Heyman scored 31 points, and Hawkins scored 21.

The Pipers concluded their regular season on April 3 with a 109–101 loss to the Colonels in Kentucky. The loss gave the Pipers a 36-42 record, good for fourth place in the Eastern Division. The team had won just 12 of its final 39 regular-season games.

In the playoffs, the Pipers faced the Miami Floridians, who had finished in second place in the division with a 43-35 record. The series opened with 2 games in Miami. On April 7, the Floridians won, 119–110. Two nights later, the Pipers rebounded with a 106–99 victory to even the series.

The next 2 games were at the Metropolitan Sports Center. On April 10, the Pipers took a 2-1 lead in the series with a 109–93 victory before 1,502 fans. On April 12, the Floridians evened the series with a 116–109 victory before 2,532.

On April 13 in Miami, the Floridians defeated the Pipers, 122–107, to take a 3-2 lead in the series, but on April 15 at the Metropolitan Sports Center, Hawkins had 33 points and 20 rebounds as the Pipers forced a 7th game with a 105–100 victory before 1,345 fans.

On April 19 in Miami, the Floridians outlasted the Pipers, 137–128, before a crowd of 5,072 to end the Pipers' season. The recap of the game in the next day's edition of the *Minneapolis Tribune* began, "In an act of mercy, Miami ended one of the most disastrous seasons—artistically and financially—in the annals of sports for the Minnesota Pipers."

Charlie Williams scored 31; Hawkins scored 22 points and grabbed 13 rebounds for the Pipers.

While the series was going on, the league announced its All-Star team. Hawkins, despite playing in just 47 games, was named to the team.

Two days after the Pipers' season-ending loss to Miami, the *Minneapolis Tribune* reported that the ABA had turned down the Pipers' proposed move to Jersey City. On May 14, the *Minneapolis Star* reported three potential locations for the Pipers franchise: Jersey City, Philadelphia and Pittsburgh.

Minneapolis Tribune columnist Sid Hartman reported on May 14 that documents submitted to the Securities and Exchange Commission in Washington, D.C., showed that the Pipers had lost $635,000 between June 1, 1968, and February 28, 1969.

On May 22, it was announced that the league office would be moved from Minneapolis to New York City. Mikan, who had a year remaining on his contract with the league, resigned in July.

In June, Hawkins, who was a free agent, and the NBA reached a settlement of his lawsuit, and he signed a five-year contract with the Phoenix Suns. He became the first ABA player to jump to the NBA. On June 27, one week after Hawkins signed with Phoenix, the Pipers officially announced they would return to Pittsburgh.

Pipers general manager Vern Mikkelsen told Sid Hartman in April that he didn't believe the team "ever got a fair chance to succeed" in Minnesota. "Rick Barry (the former NBA star who was playing with the ABA's Oakland team) didn't play a game here," Mikkelsen said. "We had counted on the duels between Connie Hawkins and Barry to draw several big crowds. But this never came off because of injuries to both. Hawkins, our top attraction, missed 35 games, and this didn't help. We tried everything to make the team go, but fate wasn't with us."

18

WALT BOND

A TOO-SHORT STINT WITH THE TWINS

O ver the course of the Major League Baseball season, ballplayers fight through an assortment of ailments and injuries. During his eleven-year professional baseball career, Walt Bond saw his share of issues.

During his rookie season with the Cleveland Indians, he was hit in the forehead by a pitch thrown by Ryne Duren of the New York Yankees. That same year, he suffered a broken ankle. In 1965, while playing for the Houston Astros, he suffered multiple abrasions and bruises and spent a night in the hospital after running into the right-field fence at Busch Stadium in St. Louis.

While playing for the Minnesota Twins' Denver farm team in the Triple-A Pacific Coast League in 1966, Bond dealt with several issues. He still managed to hit .316 with 18 home runs in 122 games with the Bears.

During spring training with the Twins in 1967, he was bothered by back pain. He had dealt with that issue periodically since 1960.

Minnesota Twins manager Sam Mele told the *Minneapolis Star* that Denver manager Cal Ermer "told me that Bond would complain everyday about something bothering him. But Ermer also said, 'stick him in the lineup and he'll hit anyway.' That's the way it's been here. He has shown me he can swing the bat, so let him complain."

There was one health issue that Bond never complained about. He played the final five years of his professional career after being diagnosed with leukemia in 1962.

Left: Walt Bond spent parts of six seasons in the major leagues. *Minnesota Twins*.

Right: Bond appeared in 10 games with the Minnesota Twins early in the 1967 season. *Minnesota Twins*.

Bond, who was born in 1937, grew up in Denmark, Mississippi, a small farming community fourteen miles southwest of Jackson. He began his professional baseball career with the Kansas City Monarchs of the Negro Leagues. During the 1956–57 baseball offseason, Bond signed with the Cleveland Indians organization.

His professional career got off to a good start in 1957. Playing for Cleveland's Cocoa, Florida farm team in the Class D Florida State League, he batted .328 with 11 home runs and 80 RBIs in 111 games. Over the next two seasons, Bond progressed through the Indians organization, batting .296 and .277.

He went to spring training with the Indians in 1960 and earned a spot on the team's Opening Day roster. With a week to go in spring training, Bond was hitting .421.

When the regular season started, he went just 5-for-30 in his first 7 games. But he went 6-for-9 in his first 3 games in May. In 2 games against the Senators in Washington, D.C., he went 5-for-6. On May 4, in the second of 2 games against the Senators at Griffith Stadium, he went 3-for-4 with 2 home runs and 4 RBIs in the Indians' 7–6 loss to the Senators, who were in their final season in the nation's capital before moving to Minnesota for the 1961 season.

According to a recap of the May 4 game in the *Washington Evening Times*, Bond "boomed a solo home run in the first inning." That home run left an impression on Senators owner Calvin Griffith. In an interview with Minnesota media six years later after the Twins acquired Bond, Griffith said his home run in 1960 "was one of the longest ever hit at Griffith Stadium."

Bond split the 1961 season between the Indians and their Triple-A farm team in Salt Lake City. In 38 games with the Indians, he batted .173 with 2 home runs.

In early 1962, Bond fulfilled his military service obligations. During that stint, he was diagnosed with leukemia. After the diagnosis, he spent most of the 1962 season with Salt Lake City. In 132 games with Salt Lake City, he batted .320 with 11 home runs and drove in 76 runs. After being recalled by the Indians in September, he put together a torrid two-week stretch at the plate. In 12 games with Cleveland, he batted .380 (19-for-50) with 6 home runs and 17 RBIs.

But Bond was sent back to the minor leagues in 1963, where he remained the entire season. He hit .276 with a career-high 25 home runs while driving in 82 runs.

On December 23, 1963, the Houston Colt 45s (the team changed its named to the Astros in 1965) purchased Bond's contract from Cleveland. A brief report filed by the Associated Press hinted at Bond's health issues. According to the brief, Bond was "purchased conditionally because he has a history of an anemic condition. The Cleveland club, however, assured the Colts he has been given a clean bill of health."

Bond flourished with Houston in 1964. He hit .254 with 20 home runs and 85 RBIs. In 1965, the team began play in the Astrodome. Playing in the more spacious domed stadium, Bond batted .263 but hit just 7 home runs while driving in 47.

In April 1966, the Houston Astros concluded spring training by playing 2 games against the Twins at the Astrodome. In the first game, on April 9, the Twins, who had won the AL pennant in 1965, defeated the Astros, 7–6. Bond made an appearance, going 0-for-1 as a pinch-hitter. The next day, he did not play in the Twins' 8–1 victory.

Before the Twins, who were scheduled to open the regular season in Kansas City on April 12, left Houston, they announced that they had acquired Bond, who had hit over .300 during the spring with the Astros, in exchange for backup catcher Ken Retzer.

Bond spent the entire 1966 season with Denver. His productive time with the Bears earned him an invitation to spring training with the Twins in 1967. In 17 exhibition games with the Twins, he batted only .194 with 1 home run and 4 RBIs. But he made enough of an impression to earn a spot on the Twins' Opening Day roster. His only home run was a 2-run blast in the Twins' 4–2 loss to the Atlanta Braves on March 31 in West Palm Beach, Florida.

After the game, Mele told the *Minneapolis Tribune*: "Bond swings a good bat. He gets his cuts at the plate. I like him in the role we've got him figured for—as a pinch-hitter."

On April 28, filling in for All-Star outfielder Tony Oliva, who was sidelined with a pulled muscle, Bond went 2-for-4 and drove in the go-ahead run in the Twins' 7–3 victory over the Washington Senators.

Over the first month of the season, Bond went 5-for-16 with 1 home run and 5 RBI, but on May 9, he was released by the Twins. For the first month of the season, Major League Baseball teams were allowed to carry twenty-eight players on their rosters. On May 10, teams needed to trim their rosters to twenty-five.

Bond told the *Minneapolis Tribune*: "What do I have to do? I hit .300. If I can't play here hitting that, I may quit. I asked why they wanted me this spring and they said to pinch-hit. Well, I pinch-hit and I play when they asked me. I don't know what they expect." As a pinch-hitter, Bond had doubled, homered and walked in 6 pinch-hit appearances for the Twins.

Shortly after being released by the Twins, Bond signed a minor-league contract with the New York Mets and was assigned to their Jacksonville, Florida farm team in the Triple-A International League.

In early June, in his first game with Jacksonville, he hit a home run. In his third game, in Jacksonville's 6–5 loss to Rochester on June 6 in Rochester, New York, he played first base and went 1-for-4 with a double.

But following the June 6 game, Bond was admitted to a Rochester hospital with "an undisclosed ailment," according to the *Rochester Democrat and Chronicle*. The newspaper said Bond "was reported in 'good' condition last night but is a shadow of his former self." In its June 9 issue, the newspaper said that "Bond had been told to go home for a rest."

Bond returned to his home in Houston. He entered a hospital for treatment, where he spent three months before dying on September 14, 1967. Bond, who had appeared as a pinch-hitter in his final major-league game on May 7 against the Boston Red Sox at Metropolitan Stadium, was one month shy of his thirtieth birthday.

Bond had an older brother named Willie. Sixteen months after Walt Bond passed away, Willie and his wife, Gloria, had a son. They named their son

Walter. Walter Bond, who grew up in Chicago, became a standout basketball player, playing for the University of Minnesota for four seasons and spending three seasons in the NBA as part of a nine-year professional career. After his basketball career, Walter Bond became a motivational speaker.

A little over three years after Walt Bond passed away, the Twins traded outfielder Herman Hill, who had appeared in 43 games in 1969 and 1970 for the Twins, to the St. Louis Cardinals. In December 1970, while playing winter ball in Venezuela, Hill drowned, on December 14, 1970. He was twenty-five.

In December 1976, Danny Thompson, who spent six and a half seasons with the Twins before being traded to the Texas Rangers on June 1, 1976, died from complications of leukemia. Thompson had played the final four years of his major-league career after being diagnosed with the disease. He was twenty-nine.

19

MINNESOTA NORTH STARS

AN EIGHTY-DAY VICTORY DROUGHT

The National Hockey League came to Minnesota in 1967, when the league, which had six franchises from 1942 to 1967, expanded by six teams.

The Minnesota North Stars began play in the 1967–68 season at Metropolitan Sports Center, which was next door to Metropolitan Stadium, home to the Minnesota Twins and Minnesota Vikings in Bloomington.

The North Stars' inaugural season was marred by the death of rookie center Bill Masterton. Early in the first period of the North Stars' game against the Oakland Seals on January 13, 1968, at the Metropolitan Sports Center, Masterton was knocked to the ice. He wasn't wearing a helmet and hit his head on the ice and was knocked unconscious. Masterton, who was playing in his 38th NHL game, never regained consciousness. He died thirty hours later, early in the morning of January 15 at the age of twenty-nine.

Masterton is the only player in the history of the NHL to die from injuries suffered in a game. After the season, the league started an annual award named after Masterton. It is presented to an "unsung hero."

The North Stars just missed advancing to the Stanley Cup Finals in the first season. They lost the 7th game of their semifinal series with the St. Louis Blues, also an expansion team in 1967, 2–1, in two overtimes.

After going 27-32-15 for 69 points in their first NHL season, the North Stars won just 18 games (18-43-15) for 51 points in their second season and missed the playoffs. The team returned to the playoffs in its third season despite one of the worst stretches of hockey in the history of the NHL.

The 1969–70 season started and finished on positive notes for the North Stars. The middle portion of their schedule was a struggle.

On December 10, the North Stars defeated the Chicago Blackhawks, 8–5, at the Metropolitan Sports Center to improve their record to 9-9-5. Over the next eighty days, the team would win just one game.

On December 29, two days after the North Stars lost, 5–3, at home to the Oakland Seals—the 8th consecutive game without a victory, which dropped the North Stars' record to 9-13-10—Wren Blair took a leave of absence as coach so he could focus on his duties as the team's general manager.

Charlie Burns, a defenseman for the North Stars, was named interim coach. NHL rules prohibited Burns from being a player-coach, so he had to hang up his skates temporarily.

Burns debuted as the North Stars' coach on December 30 in Los Angeles against the Kings. The teams skated to a 0–0 tie—the fifth consecutive tie the teams had played in Los Angeles. The North Stars went 0-2-3 in their first 5 games under Burns. That stretched the North Stars' winless streak to 13 games (0-6-7).

On January 14, four days after losing to Los Angeles, 6–4, at Metropolitan Sports Center, the North Stars defeated the visiting St. Louis Blues, 5–2, for their first victory in over a month.

But the relief was temporary. The team's next victory didn't come until March 1. Over the next 20 games, the North Stars went 0-15-5. Between January 17 and February 14, the team lost 9 consecutive games during a 0-12-1 stretch.

Through the 2021–22 NHL season, that 20-game winless streak is the eighth-longest in league history. The longest winless streak is 30 games, by the Winnipeg Jets during the 1980–81 season, their second year in the NHL. After winning the 3rd game of the season (on October 17), they went 0-23-7 over the next two months to fall to 1-25-7 on the season. The Jets finished the season with a 9-57-14 record.

On February 26, the North Stars lost, 6–2, to the Flyers in Philadelphia. That loss, which gave the North Stars a 1-17-8 record under Burns, left the North Stars with a 10-30-18 record.

On March 1, before a crowd of 14,456 at Metropolitan Sports Center, the North Stars defeated the Toronto Maple Leafs, 8–0. It was just their second shutout victory of the season. The first came in their season opener, a 4–0 victory over the visiting Flyers on October 11.

Burns provided a spark for the North Stars by playing in his first game since the loss to Oakland on December 27. In that game, Burns assisted on two of the North Stars' three goals. "I figured I had nothing to lose by suiting up," Burns told the *Minneapolis Tribune* after the game. "If we had lost, well, we've lost plenty of them before. I had thought I could help the club on the ice here and there, killing penalties and taking an occasional shift."

With Burns playing, the North Stars were able to utilize four lines against Toronto.

Bill Goldsworthy, who scored 2 goals in the victory, commented about the North Stars' improvement from their loss three days earlier to Philadelphia. "I'll never know how things can turn around like that in one day," he told the *Minneapolis Tribune*.

Burns told Sid Hartman of the *Minneapolis Tribune*: "We proved today that there isn't any reason in the world why this team shouldn't be at least third and maybe second in our division. Now that we've broken this slump, maybe we can keep going."

Rejuvenated by the victory, the North Stars went 9-5-4 over the final month of the regular season. The team won its final 4 games of the regular season—defeating Oakland, Los Angeles, Philadelphia and Pittsburgh—to finish with a 19-35-22 record (60 points) and a spot in the playoffs.

In the first round of the playoffs, the North Stars faced the St. Louis Blues. The Blues won the first 2 games of the series in St. Louis before the North Stars won games 3 and 4 in Bloomington. But the Blues won the next 2 games to win the series, 4-2.

The North Stars reached the playoffs five times in their first six seasons in Minnesota.

After the 1969–70 season, Burns returned to playing full time, playing for the North Stars for three more seasons before retiring as a player. He coached the North Stars for 42 games during the 1974–75 season.

Burns died in November 2021 at the age of eighty-five.

During the 1975–76 season, the North Stars lost 10 consecutive games to break the record of 9 straight losses during the 1969–70 season. The NHL record for consecutive losses is 18, by Pittsburgh (2003–04) and Buffalo (2020–21).

20

BILLIE JEAN KING PASSES ON BUCKSKINS' OFFER

I n May 1973, a Southern California sports entrepreneur named Gary Davidson, who had cofounded the American Basketball Association and the World Hockey Association, led a group that created a new professional sports league, World Team Tennis (WTT).

The league, which would begin play in indoor arenas in 1974, had a unique format. The teams would compete head-to-head in a 5-match contest—men's and women's singles, men's and women's doubles and mixed doubles. Each match would be 1 set.

Minnesota was named one of the sixteen franchises in the new league. Prior to the league's first player draft in August 1973, each franchise had the opportunity to sign one player in advance and then use its first pick in the draft to select that player.

For its first player, the Minnesota franchise focused its attention on the top-ranked women's singles player in the world, Billie Jean King. Before announcing the team's name, the Minnesota franchise had offered King, who earned her fifth Wimbledon singles title in 1973, a five-year contract worth $2 million. She ultimately declined the offer.

On August 3, 1973, the day of the league's first player draft, it was announced that King had signed a five-year contract worth a reported $100,000 per year with the Philadelphia franchise. "I had four teams bid for me," King told the *Philadelphia Inquirer*, "and the final decision was more than just dollars."

Len Vanelli, an executive with the Minnesota franchise, told the *Minneapolis Star*, "I just think that World Team Tennis thought Billie Jean would be better off in the east, where there were more commercial outlets."

Before reaching the agreement with Philadelphia, the New York franchise failed to reach a five-year deal with King after asking the league to subsidize part of the contract.

Vanelli described the negotiation process with King to the *Minneapolis Star*: "The deal took about 14 hours to put together. We had heard that Billie Jean had an affection for candy, so we approached the owners of a number of candy companies and worked out a major advertising campaign for her.

"The contract was for five years but payments would have been spread over 10 years and most of the $2 million would have come from commercial endorsements."

Because of more endorsement opportunities in the larger Philadelphia market, King's deal with Philadelphia was expected to be worth more than Minnesota's offer.

"Do you have any idea how much I make for doing one of those things?" King said in a magazine interview. "Even for the simplest ones, the ones that just take a couple of hours, fifty thousand bucks. Maybe seventy-five. Man, I'm not dumb. Get it while you can. I'm not going to turn down that kind of money for a few hours' work. Not when I busted my fanny all my life picking up a few pennies playing tennis."

Even though she didn't sign with Minnesota, King and Philadelphia provided one of the highlights of the 1974 season for Minnesota.

Having lost out on King, Minnesota drafted Linda Tuero in the first round of the WTT draft. Minnesota also drafted Owen Davidson, who was named the team's player-coach. Davidson had teamed with King to win the mixed doubles title at Wimbledon a month earlier.

Two weeks after the draft, the franchise announced its name: the Minnesota Buckskins.

Before the Buckskins played their first match in May 1974, the team's original investors, John Finley, Lee Meade and Vanelli, sold the franchise to a Twin Cities businessman named Burt McGlynn.

The Buckskins opened their season on May 7, 1974, at the Metropolitan Sports Center in Bloomington. In front of 2,317 spectators, the Buckskins lost to the Houston E-Z Riders, 30–28.

On June 1, the Buckskins played host to King and the Philadelphia Freedom. In front of a season-best crowd of 10,658, the Buckskins defeated the Freedom, 29–22. The loss was the first of the season for the Freedom after 12 consecutive victories. The victory improved the Buckskins' record to 8-5.

After the match, Davidson told the *Minneapolis Tribune* that King "generates enthusiasm. She has the best volley in the world, she plays hard, gets down and punches. She's got bloody everything—vitality, enthusiasm. But she isn't unbeatable."

On August 7, two weeks before the WTT playoffs were scheduled to begin, Twin Cities newspapers reported that the team was having financial difficulties. "We need a minimum of $250,000 and a maximum of $350,000 to do it [finish the season and start the 1975 season]," Meade, the Buckskins' general manager, told the *Minneapolis Star*.

When asked by a reporter what would happen if the team was unable to raise the funds, Meade responded, "Panic, I guess."

The Buckskins concluded their 44-match regular season on August 17 with a 26–17 victory over the Hawaii Leis before 1,294 at Metropolitan Sports Center. The victory gave the Buckskins, who finished in first place in the Gulf Plains Section of the league's Western Division, a 27-17 record.

The league's format for the playoffs was a 2-match aggregate-score series, with each team playing host to a match.

The Buckskins opened the playoffs on August 19 at Metropolitan Sports Center with the first leg of their series with the Houston E-Z Riders. Houston won the first leg, 28–19.

During the match, Meade announced that the league had taken control of the franchise. Meade told the *Minneapolis Star* that the league had assumed control "to meet the latest payroll." The payroll covered the previous six weeks.

"We needed about $50,000," said Meade, "and the league gave it to us. This means we have defaulted on the franchise to the league. We can reclaim the franchise by paying the league back."

The next night, in Houston, the Buckskins defeated the E-Z Riders, 29–19, to pull out a 48–47 series victory and advance to the Western Division finals against the Denver Racquets.

The series opened in Denver on August 21, with the Racquets winning the first leg, 29–18. Two nights later, before 2,547 fans at the Metropolitan Sports Center, the Buckskins won the second leg, 26–25, but Denver prevailed with an aggregate score of 54–44.

On November 6, McGlynn told the *Minneapolis Tribune* that the team would not operate in Minnesota in 1975. "There is a 50-50 chance we can sell the team to Indianapolis or Washington by November 10," McGlynn said. "I talked to the people in Indianapolis Tuesday [November 5] and the people in Washington this morning [November 6]. The league asked us to protect eight players for the upcoming draft [scheduled for November 25]. So, there will still be a team. The league also passed a resolution that everybody would come up with their dues assessment by November 1, otherwise the franchise would be terminated.

"We haven't received a letter that our franchise has been terminated. We're still negotiating with Indianapolis or Washington."

McGlynn conceded that efforts to keep the Buckskins in Minnesota through refinancing had dried up. "We were close a couple of times," McGlynn said, "but could never work things out. I went into the team as an investor. I put in $30,000, and then there were problems with other investors. So, I put in more money. Pretty soon, I was the biggest investor; I got in deeper than I planned. Basically, I'm in the bakery business, and I guess I shouldn't be in the tennis business."

McGlynn declined to say how much money he personally lost but said that the team had lost $280,000 despite finishing in the top five in the league in average attendance.

On November 18, the Indianapolis group announced that it had bought the Detroit Loves franchise. The Washington group announced that it would not purchase a franchise.

On November 25, the league announced that the Buckskins franchise had folded. The league held a dispersal draft for the players, including Davidson, Ann Haydon-Jones and Wendy Turnbull. Davidson and Haydon-Jones are members of the International Tennis Hall of Fame.

Nineteen years later, Minnesota got another look at team tennis. In the summer of 1993, the Minnesota Penguins was one of the five new teams added by the WTT. The season was shorter than the 44-match schedule in 1974, with 14 matches scheduled to be played between the end of Wimbledon in early July and the start of the U.S. Open in mid-August.

Another difference for the Penguins, whose roster included Edina native Ginger Helgeson, was that their matches were played outdoors on clay. Their home matches were scheduled to be played at the Flagship Athletic Club in suburban Eden Prairie. The club's clay surface was the only clay surface in the league.

On July 9, the Penguins opened their season with a 28–24 loss to Newport Beach (California) before an estimated crowd of 1,000. The Penguins went 6-8, finishing in fourth place in the West Division behind Newport Beach (13-1), Sacramento (12-2) and Phoenix (8-6). The Penguins, who did not advance to the playoffs, averaged 1,468 fans for their seven home matches. Their average was the lowest among the league's fourteen teams.

The Penguins, like the Buckskins, lasted just one season in Minnesota. In January 1994, the Penguins announced that the franchise had been sold to a pair of Charlotte, North Carolina businessmen for $60,000. The franchise had been run by the Minneapolis office of the International Management Group (IMG).

"We definitely were disappointed with the support we got," WTT executive director Ilana Kloss told the *Minneapolis Star Tribune*. "I don't know it was the fault of the economy or what. We thought it would be one of our strongest franchises."

Kloss said IMG had approached the league about relocating the team.

Barbara Brookes, Penguins general manager and vice president of IMG in Minneapolis, told the *Star Tribune*, "We are grateful to all our sponsors and fans for their support and we are hopeful that a WTT franchise can return to Minnesota in the future."

In 2022, the league was still in operation with five teams. The league, which played in single locations during the 2020 and 2021 seasons due to the COVID-19 pandemic, announced on its website in July 2022 that it was looking to add multiple expansion teams for the 2023 season.

21

KEN LANDREAUX

A LONG-STANDING RECORD

In 1961, the Minnesota Twins were in their first season in the state after moving from Washington, D.C., and outfielder Lenny Green was in his fifth major-league season.

Green, who was twenty-eight, had been acquired by the Washington Senators in 1959 from the Baltimore Orioles. In 1960, the left-handed-hitting Green batted a team-best (among regulars) .294 for the Senators.

From May 1 to May 28, 1961, Green put together a 24-game hitting streak. That streak stood as the Twins' record for nineteen years.

Green's record was broken in May 1980 by Ken Landreaux, who hit safely in 31 consecutive games. Landreaux's streak, which had several moments of doubt, particularly as he neared Green's record, was still the team record in 2022.

Since the 1980 season, there have been eleven hitting streaks of at least 20 games by a Twins player. The longest was 25 games by Brian Harper in 1990. Since then, the longest streak has been 24 games. That was accomplished by Brian Dozier twice, in 2016 and 2018.

In 1980, the left-handed-hitting Landreaux was in his second season with the Twins and fourth in the major leagues. Landreaux, twenty-five, was one of four players acquired by the Twins from the California Angels in February 1979 in the trade that sent Rod Carew to the Angels.

Landreaux grew up in the Los Angeles suburb of Compton. After his senior year at Dominguez High School, he was selected by the Houston Astros in the eighth round of Major League Baseball's Amateur Draft.

In 1980, Ken Landreaux set a Minnesota Twins team record for longest hitting streak. Through the 2022 season, the record still stands. *Minnesota Twins.*

Landreaux didn't sign with the Astros and enrolled at Arizona State University.

As a freshman for the Sun Devils, he batted .243. He improved to .326 as a sophomore and as a junior batted .413. During his sophomore and junior seasons, the Sun Devils, whose roster included future major-leaguers Floyd Bannister, Chris Bando and Bob Horner, advanced to the College World Series in Omaha, Nebraska.

Arizona State coach Jim Brock told the *Minneapolis Tribune* that Landreaux was "the most complete player we've ever had."

After his junior season in 1976, the Angels selected Landreaux with the sixth pick of the first round of the Amateur Draft. The Angels sent Landreaux to their Class AA farm team in El Paso, Texas. In 21 games with El Paso in 1976, he batted .220.

Landreaux started the 1977 season at El Paso but was promoted by the Angels to their Class AAA farm team in Salt Lake City after he hit 16 home runs and drove in 59 runs in 57 games with El Paso. In 62 games with Salt Lake City, he hit .359 with 11 home runs and 57 RBIs.

That earned Landreaux, who was named the Angels' Minor League Player of the Year for 1977, a promotion to the major leagues. He made his major-league debut on September 11, 1977. In 23 games with the Angels after being recalled, he batted .250.

He spent the 1978 season with the Angels, batting just .223 in 93 games.

In his first season with the Twins in 1979, Landreaux emerged as a solid major-league hitter. He played in 151 games for the Twins, hitting .305 with 15 home runs, 83 RBIs and 10 stolen bases. He led the Twins in batting average and hits (172) and was second on the team in home runs, RBIs and stolen bases.

The 1980 season started quietly for the Twins and Landreaux. On April 12, in the third game of the season, he went 4-for-5 with 2 doubles and 1 home run in the Twins' 6–0 victory over the Athletics in Oakland. But through 13 games, the Twins had a 6-7 record and Landreaux was hitting .269 with 1 home run and 2 RBIs.

Landreaux's streak began on April 23. In the Twins' 17–0 loss to the Angels at Metropolitan Stadium, he went 1-for-4, getting a double in the bottom of the ninth inning to break up Bruce Kison's no-hitter. Kison finished with a 1-hit shutout.

During the first 11 games of the streak, Landreaux had 3 hits in a 20–11 victory over Oakland on April 27 and went 4-for-5 in a 9–6 loss to the Yankees.

On May 4, in the final game of a 12-game homestand, Landreaux extended his hitting streak to 10 games by going 2-for-2 in the Twins' 10–1 loss to the Yankees.

The next night, the Twins opened a 9-game road trip in Baltimore, with Landreaux going 1-for-4—he hit a single in his first at bat—in the Twins' 4–2 victory. Landreaux was not in the lineup the next night and was not in the Twins' starting lineup in the series finale against the Orioles on May 7. According to published reports, he had been benched by Twins manager Gene Mauch. Mauch told the *Minneapolis Tribune* he was "unhappy with Landreaux's pre-game warm up" before the second game in Baltimore.

In the eighth inning of the series finale, Mauch had Landreaux pinch-hit for Dave Edwards. Landreaux drew a walk and remained in the game as the left fielder in the Twins' 8–6 loss to the Orioles. Even though he did not get a hit in his only at bat of the game, his hitting streak did not end.

According to "Guidelines for Cumulative Performance Records," Rule 9.23b in Major League Baseball's rule book: "A consecutive-game hitting streak shall not be terminated if all of a batter's plate appearances (one or more) in a game result in a base on balls, hit batsman, defensive interference or obstruction or a sacrifice bunt. The streak shall terminate if the player has a sacrifice fly and no hit."

After an off-day for the Twins, Landreaux resumed his hitting streak by going 1-for-4 in the Twins' 5–2 loss to the Yankees at Yankee Stadium. He hit safely in each of the remaining 5 games of the road trip to extend the streak to 17 games. The Twins returned to Minnesota for a brief 3-game homestand against the Milwaukee Brewers.

Landreaux had at least 2 hits in each of the 3 games as his streak reached 20 on May 18. Within 4 games of the team record, Landreaux told reporters he wasn't thinking about breaking the record. His reluctance stemmed from the threat of a looming players' strike.

The players had set a strike deadline of midnight on Thursday, May 22. As the deadline grew closer, federal mediator Kenneth Moffett told the Associated Press: "Unless there is a complete change of heart, we're headed pell mell for a strike. We're in deep trouble."

Landreaux told the *Minneapolis Star*: "And that's why I'm not even thinking about any record. Even if I get a hit in each of the next three games [which would put the streak at 23 at the strike deadline], it will be just luck if I tie the record after a strike. If we strike, and it doesn't matter how long, it will take me at least two weeks to get my batting eye back and get into the kind of hitting groove I'm into now."

The strike was averted at the last minute when a settlement was reached between the players and owners early Friday morning, May 23.

Landreaux hit safely in each of 3 games against the Chicago White Sox leading up to the strike deadline to reach 23 games. On May 23, in Milwaukee, Landreaux singled in the sixth inning of the Twins' 5–0 loss to the Brewers to tie the team record.

Landreaux broke the record the next night in a 4–0 loss to the Brewers. The Twins didn't get a hit in the first four innings off Brewers starter Moose Haas before Landreaux led off the fifth inning with a single to right. It was just 1 of 4 hits for the Twins.

After producing a hit in his 25th consecutive game, Landreaux told reporters: "It's nice to get the record, but it doesn't mean that much to me right now. Maybe later on in life, I'll look back and enjoy it more." Landreaux finished the series in Milwaukee by going 1-for-4 on May 25.

The Twins returned home for a 12-game homestand, and Landreaux hit safely in each of the first 4 games to reach 30 consecutive games. On Friday, May 30, Landreaux went hitless in his first 3 at bats before doubling in the seventh inning to extend the streak to 31.

The next day, his streak came to an end when he went 0-for-4 in the Twins' 11–4 loss to the visiting Baltimore Orioles. After he flied out to left in the eighth inning, the crowd of 8,288 acknowledged his streak with an ovation. Landreaux tipped his cap to the fans from the dugout steps.

"Day games following night games always get me," Landreaux told reporters after the game. "I'm a late sleeper. I'm a little tired, but that is no reason not to hit some of the pitches he [Scott McGregor] threw me. I don't care if I was dog-tired. I should have hit some of those pitches."

When the streak ended, it was the eighteenth-longest in Major League Baseball history. During the streak, Landreaux batted .374 (49-for-131) with 2 home runs and 19 RBIs to raise his season batting average to .344.

Landreaux vowed to put together another long hitting streak. "I'm going to do it again before it's over. I'm just glad I did it at 25 instead of 35," Landreaux told reporters. "I just wanted to show I could do it now. I'd just give it another shot. That's all I can say. They've still got to throw the ball over the plate."

Landreaux finished the 1980 season with a .281 batting average and 7 home runs and 62 RBIs in 129 games.

During spring training in 1981, Landreaux was traded to the Los Angeles Dodgers for Mickey Hatcher and two other minor-leaguers.

Twins executive vice-president Howard Fox told the *Minneapolis Tribune*, "Over the years, we have felt that we were too left-handed with not enough right-handed power. Everyone knows we've been looking for a right-handed power hitter."

Mauch, who resigned as the Twins manager in August 1980, said, "There are very few players in the American League as talented as Ken Landreaux."

Landreaux played for the Dodgers for seven seasons. In his first season in Los Angeles, the team won the World Series, with Landreaux catching the final out. The Dodgers won two more division titles in the next six seasons.

He batted at least .280 and stole at least 30 bases for the Dodgers in the 1982 and 1983 seasons. He hit a career-high 17 home runs in 1983 as the Dodgers won the NL West Division.

He became a free agent after the 1987 season. In June 1988, he signed a minor-league contract with the Baltimore Orioles. He spent the rest of the season with the Orioles' Rochester farm team in the Triple-A International League. In 1989, he played for the Dodgers' Triple-A Albuquerque team, hitting .243 in 56 games. He retired after the 1989 season at the age of thirty-five.

22

TERRY FELTON

THE FIRST WIN IS THE HARDEST

Early in the 1984 baseball season, Twins rookie pitcher Ed Hodge was bidding for his first major-league victory.

The twenty-six-year-old left-hander, who was in his sixth professional season, had started the season with Toledo, the Twins' Triple-A farm team in the International League. Hodge was 2-0 with a 2.01 ERA in 3 starts for Toledo when he was recalled by the Twins on April 26.

Hodge made his major-league debut on May 1, when he was the Twins' starting pitcher against the Mariners in Seattle. Hodge allowed 4 earned runs in five innings but didn't get a decision in the Twins' eventual 11–8 loss to the Mariners.

Five days later, Hodge made his second start for the Twins against the Oakland Athletics at the Metrodome in Minneapolis. Hodge allowed just 2 runs and six hits in seven innings before being replaced by reliever Ron Davis in the top of the eighth inning.

In the eighth, the Athletics scored a run to pull within 4–3 and had the potential tying run at third base before Davis got the 3rd out. In the ninth, Davis retired the Athletics in order to save Hodge's first career victory.

Instead of remaining in the dugout for the final two innings, Hodge retired to the Twins' locker room. "I started to watch a little bit in the dugout and then I had to come inside," Hodge told the *Minneapolis Star Tribune*. "Having the first one be like this, you know, I've got all the confidence in the world in RD (Davis) but first, I had to get in and shower."

Left: Terry Felton was the Minnesota Twins' second-round draft choice in 1976. *Minnesota Twins*.

Right: Felton made his major-league debut at twenty-one and spent parts of four seasons with the Twins. *Minnesota Twins*.

Davis certainly understood Hodge's anxiety. "The first one is always the hardest one to come by," Davis told the *Star Tribune*. "You can ask Terry Felton."

It wasn't surprising that Davis brought up Felton as a comparison. While Hodge went on to earn 3 more victories for the Twins in 1984, his only season in the major leagues, Felton was a former Twins pitcher who never won a game during his major-league career with the team.

Felton's career was captured in this headline in the August 15, 1982 edition of the *Star Tribune*: "You Win Some and Lose Some. (Unless You're Poor Terry Felton)."

In parts of four seasons with the Twins between 1979 and 1982, Felton, a right-handed pitcher, made 55 appearances for the Twins. Forty years later, his name is still attached to three major-league records for pitching futility.

Felton holds records for most consecutive losses to start a career (16), most career losses without a victory (16) and most innings pitched without a victory (138⅓). In 1982, Felton went 0-13 for the Twins. Anyone pitching for the 1982 Twins risked a losing streak, as the team finished last in the seven-team American League West Division with a 60-102 record.

Felton's won-loss record in 1982 is the last time a major-league pitcher had no victories and at least 12 losses in a season.

The Twins selected Felton in the second round, the thirty-fourth player overall, of the 1976 Amateur Draft. The Twins' first-round selection in the draft and tenth overall was Jamie Allen, a high school third baseman from Yakima, Washington. Allen did not sign with the Twins and instead played college baseball at Arizona State.

Felton was a standout pitcher during his high school career in Baker, Louisiana. Felton was 21-5 in his high school career. He was 10-0 as a junior; as a senior, he was 6-1 with a 0.68 ERA, a no-hitter and a 1-hitter. He also batted .474 with 4 home runs.

After signing with the Twins, he began his professional career with Elizabethton in the Rookie Appalachian League. In 14 appearances in his rookie season, he was 2-6 with a 3.83 ERA and 91 strikeouts in 87 innings.

In 1977, Felton bypassed the next level on professional baseball's ladder, Class A, when the Twins assigned him to Orlando of the Class AA Southern League. In 23 starts, he was 8-9 with a 3.39 ERA. He threw 4 complete games and pitched his first professional shutout.

In 1978, he was assigned to Toledo. Despite being only twenty years old—almost five years younger than the average age of the International League's players—Felton showed his potential by going 9-9 with a 3.50 ERA and 7 complete games and 1 shutout in 24 starts.

In 1979, Felton went to training camp with the Twins. His spring got off to a good start, as he and seven other Twins pitchers combined on a no-hitter in the team's 6–0 victory over Rollins College on March 7 in their first exhibition game.

He followed that with three shutout innings against the Toronto Blue Jays on March 13. In all, Felton appeared in 4 exhibition games and was 0-1 with a 7.20 ERA in nine and two-thirds innings before being sent to the Twins' minor-league camp in late March.

He began the 1979 season at Toledo. After going 7-10 with 8 complete games, 3 shutouts and a 3.42 ERA for Toledo, he was recalled by the Twins in September.

On September 28, in the third-to-last game of the season, Felton made his major-league debut. He pitched two shutout innings in the Twins' 10–1 loss against the Milwaukee Brewers at Metropolitan Stadium.

Following the 1979 season, Felton pitched winter ball in Puerto Rico. He joined the Twins again for spring training in 1980 and had a good spring. He allowed just 1 run (unearned) in his first twelve innings of spring training to earn a spot on the Twins' Opening Day roster. Twins manager Gene Mauch said he considered Felton the No. 3 starter behind Jerry Koosman and Geoff Zahn.

Felton made his first major-league start on April 14. In the Twins' 5–3 victory over the California Angels in Anaheim, he allowed 3 runs and 6 hits in seven innings. The Twins trailed 3–0 when he left game before rallying with 1 run in the eighth and 4 in the ninth.

Four days later, his losing streak started. He started against the Mariners in Seattle and allowed 3 runs in five and one-third innings as the Mariners won, 3–2.

His third start—and second loss—came five days later when he didn't get out of the first inning in the Angels' 17–0 victory over the Twins at Metropolitan Stadium. The game is also remembered for the 1-hitter by the Angels' pitcher Bruce Kison. Kison's bid for a no-hitter ended with 1 out in the ninth inning when Ken Landreaux began a team-record 31-game hitting streak with a double.

Felton fell to 0-3 on April 28 after he walked 4 and allowed 5 runs—just 1 earned—in three and two-thirds innings in the Twins' 6–4 loss to Seattle at Metropolitan Stadium.

After allowing 3 runs in a one-inning relief appearance against the New York Yankees on May 2 at Metropolitan Stadium, Felton was sent to Toledo. He spent the rest of the season with Toledo, going 7-8 with a 4.01 ERA in 25 games.

He returned to Toledo in 1981. Splitting his time between relieving and starting—he made 16 starts and 16 relief appearances—Felton went 7-11 with a 4.19 ERA. As a starter he had 6 complete games and pitched 1 shutout, and he had 1 save as a reliever. He was recalled by the Twins in September and made just 1 appearance for the team, allowing 6 runs in one and one-third innings in the 16–5 loss to Milwaukee on September 4 at Metropolitan Stadium.

In 1982, the Twins began play in their new home in downtown Minneapolis, the Metrodome. Felton made the Opening Day roster.

He got off to a good start in 1982. He was the losing pitcher in his first start of the season, April 17 at California. In his next outing, he pitched four hitless innings of relief. On April 25, he took his second loss of the season when he gave up a solo home run in the eleventh inning of the Twins' 5–4 loss to Seattle. Two days later, he pitched four and two-thirds shutout innings of relief.

In early May, he was the losing pitcher in back-to-back starts, allowing 10 earned runs in ten innings in the two games to fall to 0-4.

Over his next 5 appearances—all as a reliever—he allowed just 3 earned runs in eighteen and two-thirds innings to bring his ERA to a season-low 3.88.

On May 29, he started against the New York Yankees and allowed just 2 runs in five and one-third innings but got no decision in the Twins' 6–4 loss.

Felton's outing was highlighted by a unique occurrence, Bobby Murcer and Graig Nettles led off the top of the second inning for the Yankees with singles off Felton. But Felton ended the inning with a rare triple play. With a 3-2 count on former Twin Roy Smalley, Murcer and Nettles were moving as Felton delivered the pitch. When Smalley swung and missed, both base runners were eventually tagged out.

Twins manager Billy Gardner, who was in his thirty-eighth season of professional baseball, told reporters after the game that the triple play was the "first one I've ever seen with the batter striking out."

Felton earned his first career save on June 4, when he struck out 6 in three and one-third innings in the Twins' 6–0 victory over the Baltimore Orioles at the Metrodome.

He was the losing pitcher in 3 consecutive appearances in late June to fall to 0-8 before earning his 2nd save by pitching three and one-third innings in the Twins' 12–5 victory over the Chicago White Sox.

On August 14, Felton fell to 0-11 on the season and 0-14 in his career when he was the losing pitcher in the Minnesota's 6–3 loss to the California Angels at the Metrodome.

Felton entered the game with 2 outs in the top of the sixth with the Twins leading 3–1 and got the final out. In the top of the seventh, Felton struck out Rod Carew to start the inning, but a single, followed by an out and a walk, gave the Angels two runners on with 2 outs. A single by Doug DeCinces scored a run to pull the Angels within 3–2. With Reggie Jackson coming to the plate, left-hander Jeff Little replaced Felton and walked Jackson to load the bases. Davis replaced Little and surrendered a grand slam to Don Baylor.

Felton's 14th consecutive loss broke the record of 13 set in 1914 by Guy Morton. Morton, who was a rookie in 1914, lost the first 13 decisions of his career but finished the season with a 1-13 record. His major-league career lasted eleven years, and he finished with a 98-86 career record.

Up to that point in the season, Felton had a 4.84 ERA and 3 saves in one hundred and one-third innings. He had allowed only 82 hits, but 18 of them were home runs, and 5 of those had been game-winning home runs.

Gardner told the *New York Times*: "He's got a good arm. But most of the hitters in the major leagues are high-ball hitters. He makes too many high, bad pitches."

Twins pitching coach Johnny Podres, who was the MVP of the 1955 World Series and won 141 games in his fifteen-season major-league career, agreed with Gardner. "Terry Felton has stuff as good as anybody in the major leagues. He's pitched in games and been outstanding. They couldn't touch him. But he's got to think low every time he throws a pitch. If we thought the next time out there he'd get another loss, we wouldn't bring him in."

Podres added, "You get into trouble like his and you go out there on the mound and wait for things to happen to you, and they usually do."

On August 15, four days after breaking the record, Felton made his first start since May 29. Despite allowing just 1 earned run and 2 hits in five and one-third innings, he was the losing pitcher in the 10–2 loss to Seattle.

His final loss came on September 12, when he allowed 4 runs in one and two-thirds innings in Minnesota's 18–7 loss to the Royals in Kansas City.

He made two more relief appearances in 1982, allowing 2 earned runs in six innings. In what would be his final major-league appearance, Felton allowed 1 earned run and walked 4 in four innings against the Blue Jays in Toronto.

For the season he was 0-13 with a 4.99 ERA in 48 appearances. In 117⅓ innings, he had allowed just 99 hits and struck out 92, but he had walked 76.

Felton went to spring training in 1983, but in late March, he was sent to Toledo.

Twins president Calvin Griffith said the team had offered Felton his unconditional release. Felton declined and accepted his reassignment to the minor leagues. "We haven't given up on Felton," Griffith told the *Minneapolis Star Tribune*. "We feel he has a chance to win in the major leagues if he can develop a change-of-pace pitch. He is out of options. So for us to get him back, we would have to ask major league waivers. Another club could claim him for $25,000. But we are hopeful he will be a Twin again someday."

Felton spent the 1983 season with Toledo. Felton, who had pitched for Toledo in parts of five seasons, went 3-10 in 23 appearances in 1983. That gave him a record of 33-48 with Toledo.

Following the season, he became a free agent. Midway through the 1984 season, Felton signed a minor-league contract with the Los Angeles Dodgers. He made 7 appearances with San Antonio, the Dodgers' farm team in the Class AA Texas League, going 0-1 with a 7.16 ERA.

After the season, he retired at the age of twenty-seven. In nine minor-league seasons, he had a 43-64 record.

"I didn't do very well there [at San Antonio]," Felton told the *Minneapolis Star Tribune*. "My arm was still bothering me. It never loosened up. It was tight all the time and needed stretching." He told the *Star Tribune* that he had been diagnosed with tendinitis in his throwing arm in the spring of 1983.

In 1985, Felton began working for the East Baton Rouge Parish Sheriff's office as a guard at the parish prison. He worked in various divisions, including corrections, detective, narcotics and traffic, before being promoted to the department's night supervisor captain in 2007. In 2022, he still held that position.

23

ART JOHLFS

AHEAD OF HIS TIME

Interest in national rankings for high school sports grew after the September 1982 debut of *USA Today*. The nationally distributed newspaper offered weekly rankings for football and boys' and girls' basketball.

Over the next decade, demand for and availability of national high school rankings increased. The Associated Press began distributing a national prep poll, and the Student Sports Fab 50 started. With the advent of the internet in the late 1990s, interest grew even more as several websites began offering rankings.

All of these rankings were built on a foundation laid by a Minneapolis resident more than a half century before *USA Today* started offering national prep rankings.

In 1927, Art Johlfs began compiling national high school football rankings. Through his "National Sports News Service," Johlfs distributed rankings for the next fifty years before retiring.

When he started the football rankings, Johlfs was just beginning his career as a basketball coach. He went on to coach in the small rural Minnesota communities of Alpha, Cromwell, Deerwood and Plato for sixteen years before becoming a real estate agent in Minneapolis.

In 1944, Johlfs added national rankings for boys' basketball and in 1975 started national girls' basketball rankings. In addition to those polls, he provided Minnesota rankings to media members throughout the state.

Johlfs, who was born in 1906 in the southwestern Minnesota town of Fulda and attended the Minnesota boys' state high school basketball tournament for the first time in 1922, told the *Minneapolis Tribune* in 1967 that he read 425 Minnesota newspapers weekly. He said that once a team had three losses, he stopped reading that town's newspaper. He said he maintained a file of between five thousand and seven thousand box scores and newspaper game stories for every high school basketball team in the state.

Randall Korn, Johlfs's grandson, told the *Minneapolis Star Tribune* in 1988, "He had so many people sending him newspapers from all over the country so he could follow teams that his living room would be wall-to-wall newspapers some days."

Christi Korn-Finholt, Johlfs's granddaughter, told the *Star Tribune* in 2006 that she helped her grandfather with the rankings. "I spent a lot of time with my grandpa and remember as a young girl sifting through his newspaper clippings and short films to help him rate teams," said Korn-Finholt.

With that experience, Korn-Finholt went on to become the first female sports editor/reporter of a high school newspaper in Minnesota. She attended Edina High School as a sophomore and junior and was a member of the first Edina West High School graduating class in 1973.

In 1978, Johlfs retired and turned his rankings over to an Arizona-based high school sports historian named Barry Sollenberger. In 1999, Sollenberger turned the rankings over to Student Sports.

"He was extremely dedicated to sports and he took his ratings very seriously," Korn-Finholt said in 2006. "When his health was failing in the 1980s, he was concerned up to his dying day what would happen to the sports rankings."

Johlfs died in October 1988 at the age of eighty-two.

Randall Korn told the *Star Tribune* after his grandfather's death, "He stopped selling real estate, but he never lost his interest in sports."

In 2022, ninety-five years after Johlfs put together his first national rankings, *USA Today* and ESPN continue his legacy by producing national high school rankings.

24

GOPHERS, BADGERS
FOOTBALL RIVALRY

BRINGING HOME THE BACON

The University of Minnesota fielded its first football team in 1882. Fourteen decades later, the Gophers play for three of the most well-known rivalry trophies in major college football.

Arguably the best known, and the oldest, is the Little Brown Jug, which is awarded to the winner of the contest between the Gophers and the University of Michigan. The tradition for the Jug began after the teams played to a 6–6 tie in 1903 in Minneapolis.

The Gophers and the University of Iowa have played for *Floyd of Rosedale*, a bronze statue in the shape of a pig, since 1935.

The rivalry between the Gophers and the University of Wisconsin is the oldest in major-college football. The teams have met each year except one (1906) since 1890. Since 1948, the teams have played for a six-foot-long trophy called "Paul Bunyan's Axe." But the Axe wasn't the first trophy the rivals played for.

In 1930, forty years after the teams began playing each other, they agreed to play for a prize called "The Slab of Bacon." The trophy was the creation of Dr. R.B. Fouch, a Minneapolis dentist and 1914 graduate of the University of Minnesota. It was carved from black walnut and was two feet long and one foot wide. It had a raised football in the center with the word *Bacon* at each end. The football had the letter *M*, which was reversible to *W* when the slab was turned around.

The teams played for the trophy for the first time on November 22, 1930, in Madison, Wisconsin. The host Badgers ended a 4-game losing streak to

Above: The University of Minnesota and the University of Wisconsin football teams played for the "Slab of Bacon" trophy during the 1930s and 1940s. *University of Wisconsin.*

Left: Minnesota and Wisconsin have played for the Paul Bunyan Football Trophy (the "Axe") in football since 1948. *University of Wisconsin.*

the Gophers to take the trophy with a 14–0 victory before a crowd of thirty-two thousand.

The Gophers beat the Badgers, 14–0, before a crowd of fifty-two thousand in Minneapolis in 1931 to take possession of the trophy, but the Badgers reclaimed the trophy in 1932 with a 20–13 victory in 1932.

After winning the trophy back with a 6–3 victory in 1933, the Gophers retained the trophy until 1942.

Going into the 1941 season, the Gophers had won six Big Ten Conference titles and four national championships since 1933. The Gophers went unbeaten in 1941 to win another conference title and national championship. They completed the unbeaten regular season with a 41–6 victory—their 17th consecutive win—over the Badgers before 52,984 in Minneapolis.

There were only five bowl games scheduled to follow the season, and the Gophers, one of four unbeaten major-college teams, were considered for one of them (Cotton, Orange, Rose, Sugar and Sun).

But, two days after the Gophers' victory over Wisconsin, the Associated Press reported that Minnesota "isn't interested in a bowl invitation because of a Big Ten ruling. Except for that the Gophers, who haven't lost since late in 1939, probably could designate their own January 1 dwelling place."

According to Twin Cities newspapers, the University of Minnesota Board of Regents said it wouldn't consider an invitation to a bowl game for either "commercial or charitable purposes." The Gophers didn't play in their first bowl game until January 1, 1961.

The 1941 Gophers' season was also memorable because of Bruce Smith. Two weeks after the season, Smith, a Faribault, Minnesota native, was named the Heisman Trophy winner. He received the award in New York City on December 9, two days after the attack on Pearl Harbor.

In 1942, the Badgers ended their nine-year losing streak to the Gophers with a 20–6 victory in Madison. The Badgers' claim to the trophy was temporary, as the Gophers defeated them, 25–13, in 1943 in Minneapolis. But a headline in the November 21, 1943 edition of the *Minneapolis Sunday Tribune* read, "Minnesota Wins Bacon—But Won't Accept It."

The story, written by Halsey Hall, read: "Wisconsin had won it last year, and [Wisconsin coach] Harry Stuhldreher sent his emissary to the Gophers dressing room after the contest with the prize slab. But back came said emissary with hands still full and reporting, '[Gophers coach] Dr. [George] Hauser says no. He believes such trophies should be out for the duration (of the war) and won't take it.'"

That might have been the last time the trophy was on public display. The Gophers won the 1944 meeting, in Madison, 28–26, but no mention of the trophy was made in reports of the game. Subsequently, after the Badgers won the 1945 contest in Madison, there was no mention of the trophy.

The Gophers defeated the Badgers in 1946, 1947 and 1948, with no mention of the slab of bacon.

In January 1949, it was reported that "a new football trophy" would be awarded "annually to the winner of the Wisconsin-Minnesota gridiron contest."

The January 7, 1949 edition of the Madison-based *Capital Times* reported that the new trophy, "The Paul Bunyan axe, which replaces the 'old slab of bacon' was to have been presented prior to the Gopher-Badger game last fall but plans for the ceremony were interrupted by unavoidable circumstances."

The report said that the trophy, which carried "all the scores of previous Minnesota-Wisconsin football games and is decorated in the colors of both schools," would be unveiled at the Minnesota-Wisconsin basketball game in Minneapolis on January 10.

A photo of the new trophy appeared in the January 11 edition of the *Minneapolis Tribune* and showed Chuck Fenske, a member of Wisconsin's "W" club, presenting it to Cliff Sommer, president of Minnesota's "M" club.

In the first game played for the Axe, the Gophers defeated the Badgers, 14–6, in Minneapolis to retain the trophy. Starting in 1950, the Badgers took possession of the trophy until 1955.

The Slab of Bacon trophy had essentially been forgotten. Or lost. Until it resurfaced in 1994.

In July 1994, a member of the University of Wisconsin sports information staff found the trophy in a water-stained briefcase while cleaning out a storage room on the fourth floor of Camp Randall Stadium, the home field for Badgers football.

An Associated Press report about the find read: "No one at the department is quite sure why Wisconsin has possession of the Slab of Bacon, because the Golden Gophers won games against the Badgers in 1946 and 1947, just before the introduction of the Axe. It is possible that the 12-by-18-by-1-inch slab of black walnut has kicked around the [Wisconsin] Athletic Department since 1945, when the Badgers defeated Minnesota, 26–12, in Minneapolis."

Barry Alvarez, the Badgers' coach at the time, said, "We took home the bacon and kept it."

Adding to the mystery was that even though the trophy had reportedly been "missing" since 1945, the scores of each game through 1970 had been painted on the back of the trophy.

After it resurfaced, a committee was reportedly formed to decide the fate of the trophy. The committee was led by Minnesota associate athletic director Mark Dienhart and Wisconsin associate (and future Minnesota athletic director) Joel Maturi.

In 2021, Maturi told *Minneapolis Star Tribune* columnist Patrick Reusse, "I remember the Slab of Bacon committee. We never had a meeting. We had bigger issues in both athletic departments."

Maturi also recalled how the annual football game between the Badgers and Gophers almost came to an end in 2011.

The addition of the University of Nebraska to the Big Ten in 2011 gave the conference twelve teams (Penn State had joined in 1990). The conference announced on March 30, 2011, that it would split into two divisions for football and that the divisions would be labeled "Legends" and "Leaders."

Jim Delany, the commissioner of the Big Ten, said in a statement on the conference website: "'Legends' is a nod to our history and to the people associated with our schools who are widely recognized as legends—

student-athletes, coaches, alumni and faculty. 'Leaders' looks to the future as we remain committed to fostering leaders, the student-athletes who are encouraged to lead in their own way for the rest of their lives, in their families, in their communities and in their chosen professions. We're proud of our many legends and even prouder of our member institutions that develop future leaders every day."

The Legends Division included Iowa, Michigan, Michigan State, Minnesota, Nebraska and Northwestern. The Leaders Division was made up of Illinois, Indiana, Ohio State, Penn State, Purdue and Wisconsin.

The commissioner of the Big Ten, Jim Delany, "was devoted to the idea of equal competition within the divisions," Maturi, who was the Minnesota athletic director from 2002 to 2012, told Reusse. "We went through endless models and the final three they came up with didn't have us playing Wisconsin annually—in a different division and not as our protected crossover game.

"I got up and said, 'Minnesota and Wisconsin is the oldest rivalry in major college football. If I go home without us playing Wisconsin every year, I'm going to get fired.'

"Fred Glass from Indiana said, 'We can't get Joel fired,' and we settled on a model with Wisconsin as our crossover game."

The Legends/Leaders setup lasted three seasons. After the addition of the University of Maryland and Rutgers University in 2014 gave the league fourteen teams, the conference reorganized the divisions geographically and renamed them East and West. The Gophers and Badgers were placed in the West Division along with Illinois, Iowa, Nebraska, Northwestern and Purdue. Maryland and Rutgers were put in the East Division with Indiana, Michigan, Michigan State, Ohio State and Penn State.

In November 2022, the Gophers defeated the Badgers, 23–16, in Madison in the 132nd meeting between the rivals. With the victory, the Gophers retained the Axe (they had won 23–13 in Minneapolis in 2021) and evened their record in the series at 62 victories, 62 losses and 8 ties.

FIGHTING PIKE FLOUNDER IN ONLY SEASON IN THE TWIN CITIES

I n November 2001, Major League Baseball (MLB) commissioner Bud Selig announced that MLB intended to contract from thirty teams to twenty-eight for the 2002 season. The two teams reportedly under consideration were the Minnesota Twins of the American League and the Montreal Expos of the National League.

Before MLB could follow through with its plan, a Hennepin County District Court judge issued an injunction preventing the league from contracting the Twins, ruling that the franchise had to honor its lease to play in the Metrodome for the 2002 season.

Since the reprieve, the Twins, who had a winning record in 2001—their first season above .500 since 1992—have prospered on and off the field, with nine playoff appearances since 2002 and the opening of Target Field in 2010.

Across the street from Target Field in downtown Minneapolis is Target Center, the home of the Minnesota Timberwolves of the NBA. Five years before MLB hoped to contract, a Minnesota professional team that called Target Center home for one season was contracted.

In November 1996, the Arena Football League (AFL) ordered the Minnesota Fighting Pike to disband after just one season of existence.

The AFL, which was founded in 1986 and began play in 1987, was a hybrid form of football, playing on a 200-by-85-foot artificial turf field indoors with eight-man teams. The league was founded by Jim Foster, who had worked

Rickey Foggie, who was a standout quarterback for the University of Minnesota football team, played eight seasons in the Arena Football League. In 1996, he played for the Minnesota Fighting Pike. *University of Minnesota.*

in the United States Football League (USFL) and the NFL and patented the concept of "arena football."

On October 30, 1995, the AFL Board of Governors announced that the league would expand by two teams—giving the league fifteen members for its tenth season—by adding franchises in the Twin Cities and Houston. The league approved a bid by a group led by Twin Cities sports promoter Tom Scallen to purchase the inactive Mexico City franchise and move it to Minnesota and begin play in 1996. Mexico City had been awarded an AFL expansion team in 1994, but the team hadn't been in operation because of financial difficulties.

Scallen had a lengthy resume in professional sports and entertainment. He had owned the Vancouver Canucks of the NHL; the Ice Follies while he was president of the International Broadcasting Corporation, which owned the Ice Capades; and the Harlem Globetrotters. Before acquiring the AFL franchise, Scallen had tried to raise the money to bring a USFL expansion team to Minnesota for the 1984 season.

On November 10, the franchise announced that the team would be called the Fighting Pike and named Art Haege its head coach.

But Haege's abrupt departure provided a harbinger of things to come for the franchise. On a Sunday in mid-January, the Fighting Pike held an open tryout at Macalester College in St. Paul. The tryout was attended by two hundred hopefuls. After the tryout was completed but before the final cuts were announced, Haege left the campus and returned to his home in Iowa.

Scallen told the *Minneapolis Star Tribune*: "He just walked out. I said 'Where are you going?' He said, 'back to Iowa.' I said, 'call me in the morning, OK?' Instead, he sent me a fax that he was resigning.'"

Ray Jauch, who had been a head coach of three teams over fourteen seasons in the Canadian Football League (CFL), was named Haege's replacement. Jauch, an Illinois native, had a career coaching record of 127-

97-4 in the CFL. At the time he joined the Fighting Pike coaching staff, he had the third-highest victory total in CFL history. Through the 2021 season, his victory total remains sixth-highest in league history.

In late February, the team announced it had signed former Gophers quarterback Rickey Foggie. Foggie, who had been a four-year starter for Minnesota, was at the midpoint of a sixteen-year pro football career. He had spent the previous eight seasons in the CFL.

On April 6, the Fighting Pike opened their training camp at Augsburg in Minneapolis with thirty players vying for the twenty available spots on the Opening Day roster.

Besides Foggie, two other former Gophers—Tony Levine and Mike Sunvold—made the roster. Levine, who was from St. Paul, was a walk-on (a nonscholarship player) when he joined the Gophers. He eventually earned a scholarship and was a starter for the team in 1995. Sunvold, from Golden Valley, was in his second season in the AFL. He had played for the Iowa Barnstormers in 1995.

The roster included five others who had played college football at Minnesota state colleges. Among them was Jeff Loots, who was from St. Paul and starting his third season in the AFL. Loots, who had played with Milwaukee in 1994 and Iowa in 1995, was a record-setting quarterback during his career at Southwest Minnesota State in Marshall. During his career, he set eleven school records, nine Northern Intercollegiate Conference (now Northern Sun Intercollegiate Conference) records and nine NAIA Division I records. In 10 games in 1991, he passed for 4,111 yards and threw 50 touchdown passes.

Also on the roster was kicker Mike Vanderjagt, who had played one season in the CFL and one in the AFL before joining the Fighting Pike. Vanderjagt later become an All-Pro kicker for the Indianapolis Colts of the NFL.

Before opening the regular season, the Fighting Pike played an exhibition game, on April 20 against the Iowa Barnstormers in Iowa City. Led by future NFL MVP Kurt Warner, the Barnstormers defeated the Fighting Pike, 52–36.

The Fighting Pike officially opened their season in Houston against the expansion Texas Terror. In front of an announced crowd of 11,501, the Fighting Pike defeated the Terror, 36–24.

The following week, the Fighting Pike made their debut at Target Center when they played host to the Barnstormers. Playing in front of a crowd 14,840—which would turn out to be the largest of the season for the franchise—Minnesota jumped to a 20–3 lead just ten minutes into the game and led 34–31 at halftime. The Barnstormers limited the Fighting Pike to 9 points in the second half as they rallied for a 59–43 victory.

The loss was the first of eight consecutive defeats for the Fighting Pike. After losing to the St. Louis Stampede, 59–22, on May 10 in Minneapolis, the team traveled to Albany, New York, to take on the Firebirds. The Albany squad, coached by former Gophers quarterback Mike Hohensee, defeated the Fighting Pike, 85–30.

The Fighting Pike ended their losing streak with a 44–40 victory over the Connecticut Coyotes on July 5 in Hartford. Foggie's 13-yard touchdown pass to Alvin Ashley with five seconds remaining in the game lifted Minnesota to the victory.

After a 56–12 loss to the Orlando Predators on July 12 in Florida, the Fighting Pike played host to the Texas Terror on July 19. Texas, which brought an 0-10 record into the game, defeated Minnesota, 54–51, with a 50-yard field goal on the final play of the game. Foggie had completed 26 of 36 passes for 368 yards and 7 touchdowns in the loss, which left the Fighting Pike with a 2-10 overall record and winless in 7 home games. For the season, Foggie threw for 2,269 yards and 40 touchdown passes.

The Fighting Pike closed out the season on a positive note by winning their final 2 games, both on the road, to finish with a 4-10 record. On July 26, they defeated the San Jose SaberCats, 40–31, in California. In the season finale on August 3 in Tupelo, Mississippi, the Fighting Pike defeated the Memphis Pharaohs, 50–25. The game was played in front of a crowd of 4,520 at the Tupelo Coliseum, as the Pharaohs had been evicted from their home arena, the Memphis Coliseum. It was the 18th consecutive loss for Memphis, which went 0-14 in 1996.

Five days after the season ended, the *Minneapolis Star Tribune* reported that the team's "sagging attendance has put the team's future in doubt."

The *Star Tribune* noted that after drawing nearly 15,000 fans in the home opener, the Fighting Pike played the remainder of the season in front of crowds "announced at about 7,000." For the season, the team's average attendance of 8,846 ranked ninth in the fifteen-team league.

A team official told the *Star Tribune* that the team was looking into moving across the river to play at the St. Paul Civic Center in 1997. "The Target Center is interested in us, as is the St. Paul Civic Center," Fighting Pike executive vice-president Tom Garrity told the *Star Tribune*. "I'm confident we can have this product back in Minnesota next year."

On November 21, at a league meeting in Chicago, the AFL ordered the Fighting Pike and three other teams—Charlotte, Connecticut and St.

Louis—disbanded. AFL president Ron Kurpiers told the *Star Tribune*, "It was strictly a financial decision." The Fighting Pike had lost a reported $450,000 in their inaugural season.

Four years later, reports surfaced in Minnesota and Florida that the Florida Bobcats of the AFL were in negotiations to relocate to Minneapolis.

The *Minneapolis Star Tribune* reported in its October 25, 2000 edition: "The Target Center and SFX Entertainment were awarded the Arena Football League's Florida Bobcats franchise Tuesday, contingent on the Minnesota ownership group completing a deal with the team's current owners."

David Cooper, the AFL's president of communications, told the *South Florida Sun-Sentinel* in its October 26, 2000 edition that during a meeting of the league's board of governors earlier in the week in Dallas, "A group from Minneapolis made a presentation about the potential for moving an existing team to Minneapolis."

The Bobcats had averaged 2,785 fans for its 7 home games in the 2000 season. The league's average attendance in 2000—it had grown to seventeen teams—was 9,628.

But a deal wasn't reached, and the Bobcats remained in Florida in 2001. Prior to the 2001 season, the Bobcats signed Foggie to be their quarterback. When Foggie retired as a player following the 2004 season, he had played for five CFL teams and seven AFL teams since 1988.

The AFL remained in existence until 2019. Following the league's thirty-second season, the AFL, which was down to six teams, discontinued operations.

Two years after the demise of the Minnesota Fighting Pike, there was another attempt at professional indoor football in Minnesota.

In 1998, the Professional Indoor Football League was established. The Minnesota Monsters played their home games at Warner Coliseum on the Minnesota State Fairgrounds in Falcon Heights. Warner Coliseum is the popular venue for horse and cattle shows during the annual Minnesota State Fair.

The Monsters didn't complete the season. After losing their first three games, they forfeited a scheduled home game against the Colorado Wildcats on May 16, 1998. Six days later, the Monsters played the Honolulu Hurricanes in Hawaii. The Monsters, who wore the Hurricanes' road uniforms in the first half because their equipment hadn't arrived in time for the start of the game, defeated Honolulu, 44–41, for the first victory. But the league later forced the Monsters to forfeit the victory over unpaid bills. The Monsters folded on May 28.

BIBLIOGRAPHY

Books

Axelson, G.W. *Commy*. Jefferson, NC: McFarland & Company, 2003.

Barton, George. *My Lifetime in Sports*. Minneapolis, MN.: Olympic Press, 1957.

Bisheff, Steve. *John Wooden: An American Treasure*. Nashville, TN: Cumberland House, 2004.

Blake, Mike. *The Minor Leagues: A Celebration of the Little Show*. New York: Wynwood Press, 1991.

Bradlee, Ben, Jr. *The Kid. The Immortal Life of Ted Williams*. New York: Little, Brown and Company, 2013.

Christgau, John. *Tricksters in the Madhouse. Lakers vs. Globetrotters 1948*. Lincoln: University of Nebraska Press, 2004.

Davis, Seth. *Wooden. A Coach's Life*. New York: Times Books, 2014.

Fisher, Richard Charles, ed. *Who's Who in Minnesota Athletics*. Minneapolis, MN: Who's Who in Minnesota Athletics, 1941.

Green, Ben. *Spinning the Globe: The Rise, Fall and Return to Greatness of the Harlem Globetrotters*. New York: HarperCollins, 2005.

Gruver, Ed. *The American Football League. A Year-By-Year History, 1960–1969*. Jefferson, NC: McFarland & Company, 1997.

Hugunin, Marc, and Stew Thornley. *Minnesota Hoops. Basketball in the North Star State*. St. Paul: Minnesota Historical Society Press, 2006.

Johnson, Lloyd, ed. *The Encyclopedia of Minor League Baseball*. Durham, NC: Baseball America, 1993.

———. *The Minor League Register*. Durham, NC: Baseball America, 1994.

Kirchberg, Connie. *Hoop Lore: A History of the National Basketball Association*. Jefferson, NC: McFarland & Company, 2007.

McGuff, Joe. *Winning It All: The Chiefs of the AFL*. Garden City, NY: Doubleday & Company, 1970.

Nelson, Murry R. *The National Basketball League. A History, 1935–1949*. Jefferson, NC: McFarland & Company, 2009.

Nowlin, Bill, and Emmet Nowlin, eds. *20-Game Losers*. Phoenix, AZ: Society for American Baseball Research, 2017.

Rippel, Joel. *Dick Siebert: A Life in Baseball*. St. Cloud, MN: North Star Press, 2012.

———. *Minnesota Sports Almanac*. St. Paul: Minnesota Historical Society Press, 2006.

Schumacher, Michael. *Mr. Basketball: George Mikan, the Minneapolis Lakers and the Birth of the NBA*. New York: Bloomsbury USA, 2007.

Selko, Jamie. *Minor League All-Star Teams, 1922–62*. Jefferson, NC: McFarland & Company, 2007.

Snelling, Dennis. *The Pacific Coast League. A Statistical History, 1903–1957*. Jefferson, NC: McFarland & Company, 1995.

Spink, Alfred H. *The National Game, Second Edition*. Carbondale: Southern Illinois Press, 2000.

Sullivan, Neil J. *The Minors*. New York: St. Martin's Press, 1990.

Thompson, S.C. *All-Time Rosters of Major League Baseball Clubs*. New York: A.S. Barnes and Company, 1967.

Wilbert, Warren. *The Arrival of the American League*. Jefferson, NC: McFarland & Company, 2007.

Wolf, David. *Foul! The Connie Hawkins Story*. New York: Warner Paperback Library, 1972.

Wooden, John. *They Call Me Coach*. New York: McGraw Hill, 2003.

Articles

Cope, Myron. "The Big Z and His Misfiring Pistons." *Sports Illustrated*, December 18, 1967, 26.

Rainey, Chris. "Doc Hamann." SABR Baseball Biography Project. www.sabr.org.

Rice, Steven V. "Jack Lelivelt." SABR Baseball Biography Project. www.sabr.org.

———. "Perry Werden." SABR Baseball Biography Project. www.sabr.org.

———. "Spencer Harris." SABR Baseball Biography Project. www.sabr.org.

Rippel, Joel. "Minneapolis Millers." *The National Pastime: Baseball in the North Star State*. SABR, 2012.

Websites

Ancestry. www.ancestry.com.

Astros Daily. www.astrosdaily.com.

Baseball Almanac. www.baseball-almanac.com.

Baseball Fever. www.baseball-fever.com.

Baseball Reference. www.baseball-reference.com.

Basketball Reference. www.basketball-reference.com.

Big Ten Conference. www.bigten.org.

Encyclopedia Britannica. www.britannica.com.

Find a Grave. www.findagrave.com.

Harlem Globetrotters. www.harlemglobetrotters.com.

Hockey Database. www.hockeydb.com.

Hockey Reference. www.hockey-reference.com.

Major League Baseball. www.mlb.com.

Minneapolis Star Tribune. www.startribune.com.

Minnesota Daily. www.mndaily.com.

Minnesota Fun Facts. www.minnesotafunfacts.com.

Naismith Memorial Basketball Hall of Fame. www.hoophall.com.

Newspapers.com. www.newspapers.com.

Paper of Record. www.paperofrecord.com.

Retrosheet. www.retrosheet.org.

Society for American Baseball Research. www.sabr.org.

St. Catherine University Athletics. www.stkatesathletics.com.

Stew Thornley. www.stewthornley.net.

St. Paul Pioneer Press. www.twincities.com.

St. Paul Tennis Club. www.saintpaultennisclub.com.

USA Today High School Sports. www.usatodayhss.com.

Wikipedia. www.wikipedia.com.

Wimbledon. www.wimbledon.com.

World Team Tennis. www.wtt.com.
Zenith City. www.zenithcity.com.

Other Sources

Minnesota Fighting Pike Media Guide. 1996.
Minnesota Twins Media Guide. 1967.
University of Minnesota Football Media Guide. 2022.
University of Minnesota Men's Basketball Media Guide. 2021–22.

ABOUT THE AUTHOR

Joel Rippel is a news assistant for the *Star Tribune* in Minneapolis. A graduate of the University of Minnesota, he has worked for newspapers for nearly forty years and is the author or coauthor of eleven books on Minnesota sports history. As a member of the Society for American Baseball Research (SABR), he has contributed as a writer or editor to two dozen books published by SABR. He lives in Minneapolis and can be reached at joelrippel@hotmail.com.

Visit us at
www.historypress.com